# Understanding Workplace Violence

# Understanding Workplace Violence

*A Guide for Managers and Employees*

Michele A. Paludi
Rudy V. Nydegger
Carmen A. Paludi Jr.

Westport, Connecticut
London

**Library of Congress Cataloging-in-Publication Data**

Paludi, Michele Antoinette.
    Understanding workplace violence : a guide for managers and employees /
Michele A. Paludi, Rudy Nydegger, Carmen A. Paludi Jr.
        p. cm.
    Includes bibliographical references and index.
    ISBN 0–275–99086–9 (alk. paper)
    1. Violence in the workplace.   I. Nydegger, Rudy   II. Paludi, Carmen A.
III. Title.
    HF5549.5.E43P35   2006
    658.4'73—dc22        2006022940

British Library Cataloguing in Publication Data is available.

Library of Congress Catalog Card Number: 2006022940

ISBN: 0–275–99086–9

First published in 2006

Praeger Publishers, 88 Post Road West, Westport, CT 06881
An imprint of Greenwood Publishing Group, Inc.
www.praeger.com

Printed in the United States of America

The paper used in this book complies with the
Permanent Paper Standard issued by the National
Information Standards Organization (Z39.48–1984).

10  9  8  7  6  5  4  3  2

To those whose lives have been affected by workplace violence and to the memory of those who did not survive it.

# Contents

# Preface

During the course of writing this book, approximately two million workplace assaults occurred in the United States, sixteen million workers were sexually harassed, and 13,000 women employees were victimized at their job by a current or former mate/spouse.[1] No occupation is immune from workplace violence although there are some occupations that are at increased risk. For example, hospital employees are at high risk for experiencing violence in the workplace.[2] Assaults occur when service is denied, when a patient is involuntarily admitted, or when a nurse sets limits on eating, drinking, or the use of tobacco and alcohol. Other employees who are at high risk of workplace violence are those who exchange money with the public, for example, convenience store clerks, and those who deliver passengers, for example, taxi drivers.[3] Seventy-six percent of all workplace homicides are committed with a firearm.[4]

These statistics are alarming. The actual incidents are even more startling. For example:

- In January 2006, Jennifer Sanmarco, a former postal worker in Goleta, California, shot five people before killing herself. She had been on medical leave due to psychological problems for two years. However, she was able to get inside the fenced and guarded area surrounding the postal facility. She took an employee's electronic identification badge at gunpoint.
- In June 2005, David Wilhelm entered the EPAC plastics plant in Savoy, Texas, and killed his estranged wife and her male co-worker, Felipe de Leon, before shooting himself. The Wilhelms were in the process of divorcing.

+ In May 2005, *Primetime* (ABC) reported that Doug Williams, an employee at the Lockheed aircraft plant in Meridian, Mississippi, had made death threats and taunted African American co-workers as early as a year and half before he went on a shooting spree in July 2003 that left six dead and eight wounded. After killing his last victim, Williams shot and killed himself on the plant floor. The news program described Williams' behavior as the worst hate crime against African Americans since the civil rights movement.
+ In Miami Beach, Florida, in April 2005, Gustavo Velastegui arrived at his wife's workplace, where he shot and killed her before killing himself.
+ In July 2005, Bruce Alvin Miller, a very recently dismissed employee of Baltimore Gas and Electric Company in Maryland, shot his way into his former supervisor's office, where he killed himself.

In previous generations, employees viewed the workplace as a protected environment; one in which they felt safe. This view of the workplace no longer exists. Homicide is the most frequent cause of fatal injury for women at work; it is the number two cause for men.[5] In one of the first national studies of workplace violence, the National Institute for Occupational Safety and Health[6] noted that approximately 7,000 employees were victims of homicide in the workplace during the period 1980 to 1989. The incidence of homicide has increased in the last 16 years, according to a recent study identified by the Society for Human Resource Management.[7]

In addition, 58 percent of companies participating in this recent survey reported that disgruntled employees had threatened senior managers in the last year. Twenty-four percent of those surveyed indicated that senior managers had received in-person or e-mail threats, 17 percent said employees had intentionally and maliciously downloaded computer viruses, and 10 percent said they had been victims of product tampering.

Workplaces also suffer tardiness, absenteeism, an increased turnover rate, and decreased morale among their employees as a consequence of workplace violence.[8] Personal and vicarious exposure of employees to violence is associated with career-related, psychological, and physiological outcomes. For example, employees have reported decreased morale, decreased satisfaction with their career goals, and lowered work performance. Furthermore, employees have reported feelings of helplessness and powerlessness with regard to their career, strong fear reactions, and decreased motivation. Physical symptoms have included: headaches, sleep disturbances, eating disorders, and gastrointestinal disorders. These responses are influenced by disappointment and self-blame in response to the way others react and the stress of workplace violence-induced life changes, including disrupted career paths.[9]

The risk factors for workplace violence include psychological, behavioral, and situational stressors. For example, as organizations downsize, reorganize, and demand more of their employees, stress levels increase and contribute to workplace violence. In addition, substance abuse and poverty are contributors to workplace violence. The ease with which firearms can be obtained and the view of violence as an acceptable form of conflict resolution are other factors contributing to the increased incidence in workplace violence.

Pre-incident indicators that have been identified by research on workplace violence include the following:[10]

Increased use of alcohol and/or illegal drugs
Unexplained increase in absenteeism
Noticeable decrease in attention to appearance and hygiene
Depression and withdrawal
Explosive outbursts of anger or rage without provocation
Threats or verbal abuse directed to co-workers and supervisors
Repeated comments that indicate suicidal tendencies
Frequent, vague physical complaints
Noticeably unstable emotional responses
Behavior which is symptomatic of paranoia
Preoccupation with previous incidents of violence
Increased mood swings
Having a plan to "solve all problems"
Resistance and overreaction to changes in procedures
Increase in unsolicited comments about firearms and other dangerous weapons
Empathy with individuals committing violence
Repeated violation of company policies
Fascination with violent and/or sexually explicit movies or publications
Escalation of domestic problems
Large withdrawals from or closing an account in the company's credit union

Post-incident interviews with co-workers of employees who committed a violent act indicated that co-workers observed one of more of these indicators but considered them insignificant.[11] These employees, like most workers, were not trained by their employer in the recognition of the symptoms of potentially violent behavior or in the impact of workplace violence on individuals as well as the workplace, and they were not provided with instructions on how to report such behavior to their employer. The fact is that most individuals still cling to myths about workplace violence, including profiles of perpetrators, their own invulnerability to workplace violence, and concerns about being "whistle-blowers" to their co-workers and management.[12] Such research results show the need for educating the general public as well as management about workplace violence, its definition, incidence, explanatory models, and prevention strategies.

This book represents one response to this need—to provide an overview of workplace violence for a lay audience as well as business leaders. Scholars who study the management of organizational behavior have advocated bringing together concepts, theories, and research that may be useful to administrators in making decisions about the behavior of individuals and groups. We have adopted this approach in this book, bringing together an interdisciplinary team of authors to help identify ways in which employers must deal with workplace violence. Michele Paludi and Rudy Nydegger are psychologists; Carmen Paludi Jr. is a management consultant. All three authors work with attorneys and organizations in developing policies, investigatory procedures, and training programs regarding workplace violence and domestic violence as a workplace issue. All have taught at the undergraduate and graduate levels. In addition, the authors have published empirical research on harassment, workplace violence, and other forms of victimization. Michele and Carmen Paludi sponsored a conference for employers and human resource managers on Domestic Violence as a Workplace Issue in 2000 in Nashua, New Hampshire.

Thus, this book, while grounded in theory and empirical research, also focuses on strategies that can assist workplaces in confronting and preventing workplace violence, including the development and enforcement of effective policy statements, investigatory procedures, and sample training programs in workplace violence awareness. This book underscores the need for researchers, trainers, attorneys, human resource management specialists, and educators to work together in making employees' lives safer and based on trust and respect.

We hope you will find this book helpful in your efforts to deal with workplace violence. We encourage you to contact the resource providers we have identified for additional information related to training, research, lobbying efforts, case law, and effective management strategies.

# Acknowledgments

We thank Nick Philipson and his staff at Praeger for their commitment to us, for their assistance, and for caring about this book and the topic of workplace violence. We have enjoyed working with Nick. This is a better book because of his guidance.

Michele Paludi would like to thank Rosalie Paludi and Lucille Paludi for their dedication as sisters and as friends. She also thanks students in her winter 2006 Human Resource Management course for their suggestions and sage advice. Mel Chudzik, Dean of the School of Management at the Graduate College of Union University, deserves recognition for his support of this project.

Rudy Nydegger would like to thank Karen Nydegger for her support and excellent proofreading and editorial suggestions. He also thanks Liesl Nydegger for her suggestions and for her diligent typing and clerical support. To Ashley, Morgen, Colby, and Austin, he acknowledges their patience with the fact that Dad wasn't quite as available for fun stuff while he was writing.

Carmen Paludi thanks all the companies, organizations, and managers he has worked for, both great and not so great, who taught him the importance and the need for advocacy of a safe and stimulating work environment. While certain aspects of workplace violence can never be stopped, advocacy for nontoleration of such behavior from the highest organizational levels downward, for good and alert management skills and practices, and for an educated workforce are paramount to minimizing the impact of workplace violence.

# CHAPTER 1

# Understanding Workplace Violence: Myths and Realities

Violence is not merely killing another. It is violence when we use a sharp word, when we make a gesture to brush away a person, when we obey because there is fear. So violence isn't merely organized butchery in the name of God, in the name of society or country. Violence is much more subtle, much deeper, and we are inquiring into the very depths of violence.

—Jiddu Krishnamurti

The cause of violence is not ignorance. It is self-interest. Only reverence can restrain violence—reverence for human life and the environment.

—William Sloan Coffin

Nonviolence doesn't always work—but violence never does.

—Anonymous

Opinions founded on prejudice are always sustained with the greatest of violence.

—Francis Jeffrey

**Questions for Reflection**

- How do you define workplace violence?
- In what occupations do you believe there are the largest numbers of incidents of workplace violence?

+ Do you believe you can "spot" employees who are likely to commit violent acts?
+ Do you believe workplace violence can occur at your place of employment?
+ Do you think workplace violence is increasing? Why or why not?

---

*One day in 1995, James Davis arrived at Union Butterfield, a tool company in Asheville, North Carolina, from which he had been fired two days earlier for fighting. Davis walked into the building carrying a semiautomatic rifle and a pistol. He fired approximately 50 shots, killing three employees. When he was done terrorizing the workplace he surrendered to the police. Davis's co-workers eventually testified that he had had violent tendencies for years. For example, he had attempted to choke a co-worker. Union Butterfield did not take any security steps to prevent the crime. They did not monitor the parking lot, lock doors, or add security to the building.*

Incidents such as this one at Union Butterfield are all too common in companies in the United States and throughout the world. The National Institute of Occupational Safety and Health[1] found that violence is a major cause of death or injury on the job. Homicide is the second leading cause of occupational injury death overall (second to motor vehicle accidents) and is the leading cause of occupational death for women. The Occupational Safety and Health Administration (OSHA) reported 551 workplace homicides and 5,703 fatal work injuries in 2004.[2]

While workplace homicide is the fastest growing form of homicide, other forms of aggression occur in organizations. For example, OSHA reported in 2004 that there are approximately two million workplace assaults and that more than six million workers are threatened annually.[2] The U.S. Department of Justice[3] in 1994 reported one million workers assaulted each year and over 160,000 sustaining personal injury.

We note that the differences in incidence rates may be due to methodological variations among research studies. Some researchers have used retrospective data in collecting incidence rates, for example, asking employees about their previous experiences with workplace violence. Other researchers have asked employees about their more immediate experiences with workplace violence. In addition, direct questions about workplace violence may elicit unreliable incidence rates since individuals do not typically understand what constitutes workplace violence. Thus, random and systematic error is introduced into the procedure.

Furthermore, several measuring instruments used to collect incidence data have not been submitted to psychometric analyses, including analyses of reliability and validity. Comparing incidence rates when studies have not used an identical measuring instrument also poses a methodological problem.

Finally, cross-cultural studies may not use the same definition of workplace violence as do researchers in the United States. Thus, making comparisons of incidence rates across cultures is problematic if surveys have not been interpreted for research participants in different countries.[4]

Despite these methodological problems, there is agreement among researchers that workplace violence is increasing and must be addressed by, among other methods, developing preventative and reactive measures for dealing with it in organizations.

Reading newspapers, reading magazines, and listening to television one certainly begins to develop ideas and perspectives about workplace violence, its prevalence, its perpetrators, its victims, and its impact on the workplace and on society. The mythology that is created about this topic may help to "explain away" workplace violence or to minimize its damage to employees and employees' families. In this chapter we will show that popular myths are so pervasive that they confuse individuals about workplace violence.

## MYTHS REGARDING WORKPLACE VIOLENCE

### Myth 1: Workplace Violence Is a Rare Event.

*Reality:* According to the U.S. Department of Justice,[5] the workplace is one of the most dangerous places in America. Further, the Department of Justice reports that workplace homicide is the fastest growing type of homicide in the United States. We are confident that people are more conscious of workplace violence today, and are more likely to report it. However, most workplace violence is not reported at all. Unless workplace aggression results in lost time at work it is very unlikely to be reported and acknowledged. In fact, if an employee takes time off work and uses sick time or personal time, it may not be "officially" recorded at all.[6] Thus, the statistics that we have are very probably *underrepresentations* of the severity of workplace violence.

### Myth 2: The Post Office Is the Worst Place for Workplace Violence.

*Reality:* The phrase "going postal" implies that postal workers frequently kill people at work. Of course, there have been some tragic episodes of this, but the Post Office is hardly the most dangerous place to work, and in many ways it is relatively safe.

Most workplace violence comes from outside an organization and is not committed by people within the organization at all.[7] Most workplace violence is due to robberies and other crimes. Less workplace violence is due to business disputes and personal conflicts. We will look at these types of data in more detail later, but it is clear that the Post Office is not as dangerous a place to work as it may seem, given popular perceptions.

**Myth 3: Violence at Work Usually Affects Men—Women Are Not as Badly Affected.**

*Reality:* Workplace violence affects both men and women, but in different ways and at different rates. For example, men are more likely than women to be victims of homicide and physical assault as well as assault by a stranger.[8] Women are more likely than men to be assaulted by someone they know.[8] However, as mentioned earlier, homicide is the leading cause of work-related death in women.[9] Certainly, men are statistically more likely to be victims of violence at work, but this finding clouds the important point—women are not safer at work because of their sex. In fact, some professions that are high-risk for violence are traditionally "female." The following occupations are likely to experience workplace violence: teaching, social work, health care, other social services, and retail sales where the employee works at night, alone, and handles cash.[10] Both men and women working in these occupations have a greater chance of being victims of violence than workers in other occupations. However, since women tend to be more heavily represented in these types of jobs, they are disproportionately at risk in these situations.

It is also true that certain types of workplace violence are more likely to be perpetrated on women. Rape, sexual harassment, and stalking are clearly more likely to involve female victims. Women are more likely than men to be victims of violence when the perpetrator is known to the victim. This includes, for example, intimate partner violence that spills over into the workplace, ex-spouses seeking "revenge" by coming into the former wife's work environment, and other such situations, which we discuss in chapter 6.

**Myth 4: With Better Security and Safety Procedures, Violence at Work Will Be a "Thing of the Past."**

*Reality:* Certainly in the period since the tragedy of the World Trade Towers we might think that we are much safer from workplace violence and terrorism than we were in the past. Many organizations are becoming more aware of the importance of dealing with and preventing workplace violence. However, it could hardly be claimed that most organizations have effective policies, procedures, and training in place to handle workplace violence. Too often, executives believe that this is really not as big a problem as many people think, and that if we simply put some obvious (and probably superficial) procedures in place, then people will settle down, get back to work, and not be so affected by these relatively "rare" events.

As we pointed out earlier, these events are not really as rare as we would like to believe, and any organization that feels it is immune from the problems of workplace violence is misguided. This false sense of security has caused and will cause problems. For example, one of the authors (Rudy Nydegger) was consulting with an organization that prided itself on its high-tech, up-to-date security systems. Walking around the company premises, he noticed some interesting things that he later brought to the attention of some of the managers. At one point, he had gone to the restroom, and on the way back he put his visitor's badge in his pocket and walked up to one of the security doors. An employee whom Nydegger had never seen before opened the door with his security card, and held the door open for the visitor without even asking for any identification. Further, Nydegger noticed that some of the security doors were propped open because it was too "inconvenient" for people to have to keep using their cards to get in and out of the secure areas.

**Myth 5: People Who Are Likely to Commit Workplace Violence Are Easily Identifiable.**

*Reality:* In fact, it is very difficult to predict who will commit violent acts in the future. When we try to anticipate violence by "profiling," we risk discriminating against an individual with very little chance of being correct. For example, if we assume that we need to keep a closer eye on our younger minority employees because "everyone knows" that they are prone to violence, we shall probably be watching the wrong people. Actually, 80 percent of violent acts in the workplace are committed by white males over the age of 30. Or perhaps we might assume that our biggest threat comes from disgruntled former employees. However, only 3 percent of workplace violence comes from former employees. And once again we would be directing our attention toward people who are unlikely to cause any problems. Perhaps, then, we had best be careful of disgruntled current employees, since former employees are not such a huge risk. Once again, however, we would be missing many of the problems, since only 20 percent of workplace violence is committed by current employees.

Obviously we should be careful of anyone who comes into the organization from the outside. Two-thirds of the acts of violence in the workplace are committed by people who are outside the organization, as in the case of robberies. Consequently, trying to predict violence by targeting any specific group of people is probably going to result in substantially more incorrect guesses than correct ones.

Of course, any violence prevention program does try to target people who are likely to commit violence, but this is not easy to do. Our prevention efforts must take into account the many, complex factors that interrelate to produce violence. Simply picking people out because they appear to us to be "violent" sorts of people cannot by itself be very helpful. We return to this issue in chapter 7.

**Myth 6: When Violence Is Dealt With at Work It Does Not Spill Over to the Outside World, and Violence in People's Lives outside Work Does Not Really Impact the Work Environment.**

*Reality:* We know that when people are victims of violence at work it does affect them in many ways (see chapter 3). It is likewise true that the problems people experience outside work impact them significantly and frequently at work. Frequently, people who have problems at work or at home suffer from various psychological and emotional difficulties or even physical problems that may make it difficult for them to function normally in other settings. We cannot just "turn off" the emotions switch when we leave work or home and assume that everything will be "normal" everywhere else.

Thus, when employees are victims of violence at work, we know without question that they are affected not only at work but in all other areas of their lives as well. Too often the effects at work are very troubling and may result in the employee having to take time off, go on medical leave, or sometimes quit the job entirely. It is also true that employees' lives are very much affected outside work when they are the perpetrators of workplace violence. There may be legal, professional, personal, social, and health implications for them.

It is also true that when people have violence in other parts of their lives, it significantly impacts the work environment. As mentioned earlier, homicide is the leading cause of workplace fatality for women, and we also know that women are more likely to be victimized by someone they know—including their intimate partners,[11] as we will see in chapter 6.

**Myth 7: Workplace Violence Is Random and Unpredictable, and There Is Not Much That Can Be Done to Prevent It.**

*Reality:* In most cases, when we examine a situation after violence has occurred, we see some indicators that a problem was brewing. Unfortunately, we do not always see the signs until after the violence has occurred. The signs may be seen in employees' behavior; they may be seen in a lack of safety programs in the workplace or a failure to react to previous problems in a constructive way. It is certainly true that violence is difficult to predict in people. However, if we do what we can to deal with some of the "people problems" that might lead to violence, then we can reduce the problems to some degree. Job stress and workplace violence are recognizable, predictable, and preventable. We will never be able to eliminate all violence from the work environment. However, it is reasonable to assume that better programs, safer work environments, and better training can and should reduce the frequency of workplace violence. We discuss training programs in more detail in chapter 7.

**Myth 8: It Won't Happen Here.**

*Reality:* Most employees believe that workplace violence could never touch their lives, that it happens to other individuals who live far away, but never to people like themselves. One explanation for this myth concerns the "just world hypothesis."[12] Employees who believe in a just world believe bad things happen only to those who somehow bring on or deserve the consequences of their acts. Thus, they try to find a personal reason for an individual's selection as a victim of workplace violence. It is frightening for them to realize that it could happen to them or to someone they know. The just world hypothesis is thus a protective mechanism; it shields individuals from a range of fears.

The real risk of this myth is that when employees or employers really believe it is true, they do not engage in the prevention measures that they need in order to stay safe. Employers often will not institute safer programs or environments, especially if these prevention programs are expensive.[13] Even when employers put programs in place, if employees do not take the risk seriously, they will not pay attention to or even participate in the training or other programs that could actually make the workplace a safer environment. Unfortunately, we know that most workplace violence or aggression is not reported unless it results in lost work time.

**Myth 9: Workplace Violence Generally Means Assault or Homicide.**

*Reality:* If this were true, then workplace violence would be a relatively rare event. Most of the aggression that occurs in the workplace is verbal or indirect and passive.[14] Whether or not this should be called "violence" or not is up for debate, but it does seem that most authorities would include this type of behavior in a description of workplace *aggression* (see chapter 2). If we are to get a better sense of the nature and scope of the problem, we should probably use the most inclusive definition or description possible. Perhaps it makes more sense to refer to workplace violence *and* aggression. Even if these are not exactly synonymous, they are certainly related concepts.

Other terms that are used synonymously with workplace violence include the following: "bullying," "mobbing," "workplace harassment," "mistreatment," "emotional abuse,"[15] and "incivility."[16] While these various different forms of workplace aggression or abuse may not precisely be "violence," they probably differ from it rather in degree than in kind. We need to think of workplace violence and aggression as being on a single continuum ranging from incivility to homicide with all of the other forms of violence/aggression/abuse somewhere in the middle. This seems to be a more realistic way of conceptualizing the issue than looking at all types of violence as being qualitatively different and unrelated.

**Myth 10: Most Workplace Violence Is Committed by Employees.**

*Reality:* As we have pointed out, most workplace violence comes from outside the organization.[17] Robberies and other crimes constitute 81.82 percent of the incidents of workplace violence. In the United States, being murdered by a co-worker receives considerable attention in the press, even though this accounts for only a small percentage of workplace homicides.

Too often the culture of a neighborhood or area around an organization will intrude into an organization in ways that are not to the best advantage of the organization or its employees.[18] For example, an organization in a high crime area may be more prone to robberies, muggings, and assaults because of the nature of the environment in which the organization is located. This has created real problems for many organizations, which have felt the need to move into "safer" areas to protect themselves and their employees and customers. However, this also tends to take more jobs out of an area of high unemployment, decrease the tax base, remove some of the positive influences in the area, and continue the downward economic and social spiral that so often accompanies the woes of such areas.

Workplace violence can be committed by anyone, but to assume that organizations need to focus primarily on their employees is to miss some of the major risk factors in the workplace.

**Myth 11: Workplace Violence Is Primarily a Problem in the United States.**

*Reality:* Workplace violence is a problem all over the world.[19] It is clearly a problem in the developed countries that track this type of information, but it is also a problem in developing countries. Data from the 1996 International Crime Victim Survey demonstrated that workplace assaults occurred in such places as Western Europe, Asia, Africa, and Latin America.[19] In fact, many countries have higher rates of violence and aggression than the United States or Canada.[20]

France, Argentina, Romania, Canada, and England have the highest reported rates of assault and sexual harassment on the job.[21] Data from emerging nations are largely nonexistent, but it is clear from some reports and anecdotal information that workplace violence is a problem in these countries. There is more media coverage and there is more access to research opportunities in the more developed nations. Thus we tend to know more about them, but that does not mean that the problems are less severe in the less developed nations. To date, we simply don't know.

In the United States, we believe that workplace homicide is complicated by the availability of firearms. While this is a controversial position, the fact that the workplace homicide rate is higher in the United States. than in many other countries suggests that the easy access to firearms is at least a contributing factor. According to the National Institute for Occupational Safety and Health (NIOSH), 75 percent of workplace homicides are committed with a gun.[22] From a practical standpoint, it is necessary to keep the firearm issue in mind when developing education and prevention programs.

**Myth 12: Workplace Violence Is Largely a Problem of Inner Cities and More Dangerous Neighborhoods.**

*Reality:* Violence at work knows no neighborhood, racial, or ethnic boundaries. We do know that in high crime areas it is more likely that external crime will be brought into the workplace in the form of robbery and assault, but in no way does this minimize the problem or exempt other settings from it. To try to reduce risk by relying on stereotypes, profiling, and simplistic explanations is to open the door to crisis in organizations. Rather than trying to feel safer by looking at more dangerous areas and exaggerating their risks, we need to look at our own organizations to see what we can do to make them safer and healthier in all ways. If our organization happens to be in a high crime area, then we need to take this into account when designing safety systems. We need to have controlled access, well-trained employees, safe parking areas, and good security. If we are located in a relatively safe area we need to be aware of the same issues and the same precautions, but perhaps not in quite the same way. Every organization and every neighborhood has its own advantages and liabilities, and these need to be involved in the planning when we assess and plan for violence prevention and workplace safety programs.

## WORKPLACE VIOLENCE: PERCEPTIONS AND REALITIES

Sociologist W. I. Thomas wrote, "If men define things as real, they are real in their consequences."[23] We must remember that we do not actually respond to "reality" but only to our perception of reality. As much as we would like to believe that our perceptions are accurate reflections of the "real world," they are, at best, good approximations of what the world is and what happens within it. In fact, although no one perceives things in exactly the same way as anyone else, we seem to be able to relate to one another's experiences as if we know exactly what others have experienced. Logically we know that this isn't the case, but it certainly feels as if it is true. The reason for our ability to relate to others is that we "consensually validate" our experiences and those of others by comparing our perceptions. Then we tend to agree on interpretations of things that help us understand and explain the world in ways that make it comfortable and reassuring.

When we examine a phenomenon that is as emotionally charged as workplace violence, it is understandable that people will have strong feelings about it. We also know that our feelings often impact what we perceive, how we perceive, and how we interpret our perceptions. Thus, for all of us, to understand our perceptions we also have to understand and appreciate our emotions and how they might impact our perceptions. The perception of relative risk, for example, is often very much affected by perceptions. Often we may feel unreasonably threatened by a person we "perceive" to be menacing, when in fact the only reason the person seems to be a threat is our perception or stereotyping of him or her. On the other hand, we have often heard it said of a perpetrator of violence, "He seemed like such a nice person. I can't believe that he did such a terrible thing."

One of the perceptual phenomena of which we are aware is called as the perceptual set.[24] This is the process whereby we tend to see and hear what we expect. We can all recall situations in which we thought that we were experiencing one thing, only to find out that we had misperceived it and we were really experiencing something else. For example, when we feel that people have been rude to us, it hurts our feelings, we feel badly about it, and perhaps angry with them. Then we find out that what we thought they said was actually not what was intended, and when they explain themselves we realize they weren't being rude at all.

We tend to feel that our perceptions are accurate representations of reality, and to a large extent they probably are. However, we also have to be aware of the fact that often our perceptions will lead us away from actual reality. This can present problems. How often has workplace violence or aggression resulted from misunderstandings or faulty perceptions? There is no way to answer this question other than to assume that it has probably happened many times.

Perceptions are also involved in a phenomenon called the "self-fulfilling prophecy."[25] This occurs when an event comes true primarily because we think that it will come true. For example, suppose a worker feels that other people don't like him and that they want to hurt him. He not only believes this but he acts as if it were true. Thus, he behaves as if he feels that others don't care for him, and of course he gives this message to others, and they begin not to like him—because of the way he acts toward them. This might actually progress to the point of aggressive actions between the worker and a colleague, but the real cause is the worker's original perception that no one liked him. In other words, the "prophecy" that others disliked him and wanted to harm him came true because of his original perception.

This example shows just one way in which self-fulfilling prophecies can not only interfere with our perceptions of things but also affect events. When we are dealing with the realities of workplace violence, we must be aware of problems like self-fulfilling prophecies and their possible impact on the issues with which we are dealing.

Another psychological process that is related to violence is causal attribution.[26] Causal attribution refers to people's interpretation of the causes of their behavior and the behavior of others. At times, we see the cause of behavior as internal; this implies that people control what they do and that the "cause" of their behavior is actually inside themselves. At other times we see the cause of behavior as outside ourselves or other persons, for example, in the environment, in the stars, due to luck, and so on.

Attribution can affect violence in many ways. For example, when queried about the reasons why they might have committed violence, perpetrators will often explain their behavior by pointing to outside factors, and very often they feel that the violence they caused was fully understandable "given the circumstances." On the other side, we often explain the behavior of others by using an internal attribution. This is often called the fundamental attribution error.[27] In this situation, we look at someone else's behavior and incorrectly attribute it to some internal factor. Thus, when looking at violence we might assume that the sole cause of the violence was that the perpetrator was "crazy." Whether or not that "diagnosis" is true, it is probably not that simple.

The self-serving bias[28] refers to the way we tend to explain our failures with external attribution and our successes with internal attribution. For example, "The reason I hit that person was that he was being very annoying, and anyone would have hit him in that situation." Or, "The reason I didn't get violent in that situation but the other person did is that I am much smarter and psychologically healthier than the other person." Trying to understand the causes of violence by looking *only* at perceptions and attributions will never allow us to fully appreciate such a complex and multifaceted phenomenon. However, trying to understand violence *without* appreciating the role of perception and attribution will never be adequate either.

As we continue our quest to understand and hopefully deal more effectively with workplace violence, we will try to bring all of these factors together in a way that will help us to deal with this issue more accurately and completely.

## RESOURCES

Bowie, V., Fisher, B., & Cooper, C. (Eds). (2005). *Workplace violence: Issues, trends, strategies.* New York: Willan.

Cortina, V., Magley, V., Williams, J., & Langhout, R. (2001). Incivility in the workplace: Incidence and impact. *Journal of Occupational Health Psychology, 6,* 64–80.

Einarsen, S., Hoel, H., Zapf, D. & Cooper, C. (Eds.). (2003). *Bullying and emotional abuse in the workplace: International perspectives in research and practice.* New York: Taylor & Francis.

VandenBos, G., & Bulatao, E. (Eds.). (1996). *Violence on the job: Identifying risks and developing solutions.* Washington, DC: American Psychological Association.

National Institute for Occupational Safety and Health (NIOSH):
http://www.niosh.gov
200 Independence Avenue, SW
Washington, DC 20201

Society for Human Resource Management (SHRM):
http://www.shrm.org
1800 Duke Street
Alexandria, VA 22314

## OSHA

U.S. Department of Labor, Occupational Safety and Health Administration (OSHA):
http://www.osha.gov
200 Constitution Avenue, NW
Washington, DC 20210

## Regional Offices

**Region I (CT, ME, MA, NH, RI, VT)**

JFK Federal Bldg.
Boston, MA 02203

**Region II (NJ, NY, PR, VI)**

201 Varick Street
New York, NY 10014

**Region III (DE, DC, MD, PA, VA, WV)**

The Curtis Center
170 S. Independence Mall West
Suite 740 West
Philadelphia, PA 19106

**Region IV (AL, FL, GA, KY, MS, NC, SC, TN)**

61 Forsyth Street, SW
Atlanta, GA 30303

**Region V (IL, IN, MI, MN, OH, WI)**

230 South Dearborn Street
Chicago, IL 60604

**Region VI (AR, LA, NM, OK, TX)**

525 Griffin Street
Dallas, TX 75202

**Region VII (IA, KS, MO, NE)**

City Center Square
1100 Main Street
Kansas City, MO 64105

**Region VIII (CO, MT, ND, SD, UT, WY)**

1999 Broadway
PO Box 46550
Denver, CO 80201

**Region IX (AS, AZ, CA, HI, NV, Northern Mariana Islands)**

71 Stevenson Street
San Francisco, CA 94105

**Region X (AK, ID, OR, WA)**

1111 Third Avenue
Seattle, WA 98101

# CHAPTER 2

# What Is Workplace Violence?

When people say there is too much violence in my books, what they are saying is there is too much reality in life.

—Joyce Carol Oates

The man who strikes first admits that his ideas have given out.

—Chinese Proverb

In violence we forget who we are.

—Mary McCarthy

Nonviolence means avoiding not only external physical violence but also internal violence of spirit. You not only refuse to shoot a man, but you refuse to hate him.

—Martin Luther King, Jr.

### Questions for Reflection

- Has your definition of workplace violence changed since you've read the first chapter of this book? Why or why not?
- In which occupation do you believe workplace violence is most prevalent?
- Do you believe it is likely that domestic disputes carry over into the workplace?
- Do you believe workplace violence impacts employees' emotional and physical well-being? Their career development? Their interpersonal relationships?

* Do you think it is possible to provide a profile of individuals who are most likely to commit violent acts in the workplace?
* What would you like your employer to do to deal with workplace violence?

---

*In July 2003, Doug Williams shot and killed six co-workers and wounded eight others before committing suicide at the Lockheed Martin plant near Meridian, Mississippi. Lockheed ordered everyone to the canteen area to determine which employees were still alive. According to one co-worker, "When Lockheed ordered everyone to the canteen area, I twice had to try to find a way that did not have a body lying in the aisle." Employees filed a lawsuit stating that Lockheed failed to protect its employees by ignoring numerous complaints that Williams had threatened to shoot African American employees. They also claim that Lockheed fostered a volatile work environment and denied employee requests for security guards. Lockheed Martin spokesperson Joe Stout stated that "The shooting at the Meridian facility was a senseless tragedy to all who were affected by it, including the victims, their families, the community and all the hard-working men and women at Lockheed Martin, who, like the families, still mourn the loss of their colleagues."*

Understanding something as multifaceted and complex as the events at Lockheed Martin is certainly not an easy task. Why did Doug Williams kill co-workers? Why did Lockheed Martin not have security guards on the premises? If Williams threatened to kill co-workers, why didn't management take this statement seriously and do something to prevent the workplace violence that occurred? And, what behaviors constitute workplace violence? Threats? Emotional abuse? Passive-aggressive behavior? Or just murder? We will address these issues in this chapter, beginning with the question, "What is workplace violence?"

To understand workplace violence we must do the following:

* Understand the magnitude and effects of violence in the workplace
* Identify the potential perpetrators and victims
* Identify and implement reasonable and legitimate solutions to reduce the threat of and potential for violence in the workplace[1]

The European Commission has defined workplace violence as involving "incidents where persons are abused, threatened or assaulted in circumstances related to their work, involving an explicit or implicit challenge to their safety, well-being or health."[2] This is a very broad, general definition that covers a wide range of potential actions. Its advantage is its breadth; however, it does not give us very precise indications of the types of behaviors that would qualify as violence under this definition. Nor does it clearly indicate what might be meant by an "implicit challenge" to people's sense of safety or well-being.

In an attempt to be more specific, T. H. Shea has defined workplace violence as "any act against an employee that creates a hostile work environment and negatively affects the employee either physically or psychologically. These acts include all types of physical or verbal assault, threats, coercion, intimidation and all forms of harassment."[3] This definition spells out some of the specific behaviors that qualify as workplace violence. In addition, it refers to factors that will affect the work environment, including verbal and/or psychological threats and harassment. This definition limits itself by referring only to employees as victims.

Researchers in Australia, in an effort to more precisely define the concept of workplace violence, have offered another definition. They suggest that "occupational violence is the attempted or actual exercise by a person of any force so as to cause injury to a worker including any threatening statement or behavior which gives a worker reasonable cause to believe he or she is at risk."[4] This definition, too, seems to be precise but somewhat limiting. Even the idea of "occupational violence" seems to constrain the potential application of the concept. It also focuses on "injury," which is a difficult concept to apply when we talk about an employee reasonably believing that he or she is at risk. Nor does this definition get into what might be better described as harassment or bullying. It is implied, but not specified in a way that makes it easily understood as an example of workplace violence.

This definition does specify potential violence in the form of statements or behaviors and looks at the potential harm as being based on the employee's belief that he or she might be at risk. This is essential because violence and aggression can have effects that are relatively independent of the intentions of the perpetrators. Another way to explain this is to point out that people are responsible not only for their intentions but also for the consequences of their actions. Whether or not people "mean" to frighten or intimidate others, if their behavior has that effect, then they have some responsibility for that effect as well as for the action itself. [5]

## TYPES OF VIOLENCE AND AGGRESSION IN THE WORKPLACE

In an attempt to more clearly delineate what is meant by workplace violence, the California Occupational Safety and Health Administration (Cal/OSHA)[6] pointed out that there are basically three types of workplace violence:

- Violence occurring primarily due to robberies with the aim of obtaining something of value from the workplace, the offender having no legitimate right to be on the premises
- Violent acts committed by individuals who have a legitimate right to be on the premises as recipients or providers of services (e.g., clients, patients, students, customers, etc.)

♦ Violent occurrences that happen to involve co-workers and may also involve people in superior or subordinate positions

While these general descriptions outline the scope of workplace violence, we should also try to specify some of the basic forms of violence and aggression that we are including in our coverage of the topic. Obviously, homicide and physical assault would qualify as workplace violence in any definition. Fortunately they are not the most common types of violence and aggression in the workplace. Because they are so destructive and harmful, they must be considered to be high priority in efforts to reduce, control, and hopefully minimize or eliminate destructive acts. However, there are many other, more common examples of workplace violence and aggression with which we must deal. In fact, it is clear that these other types of aggression are even more common in the workplace and have extremely harmful effects.[7]

Some of these other forms of violence and aggression have been described using different names and concepts, but all have characteristics in common. First, all involve some act that has the intention and/or the effect of causing physical or psychological harm to another employee. Although some argue that violence against the physical plant of an organization does not fall into this category, we argue that it does. When a person causes physical damage to a building, a piece of equipment, or another physical element of the organization, this has the effect of causing concern or even fear among others in the organization and thus they are harmed as well.

Another aspect of the types of violence or aggression discussed here is that the actions in question are under the control of the perpetrator. Of course, some would argue that an individual may "accidentally" do something that threatens or scares another person in the workplace. Since it is not intentional, then it is not aggressive. However, when people's behavior appears aggressive to others, and it produces the same kinds of effects as if it had been intended to be aggressive, then the effect is the same and the perpetrator is still the cause of the perceived aggressive act. If people do something that they do not intend to appear aggressive but that is perceived as such by others, then the solution is simply to give the perpetrators feedback about the effect of their behavior and indicate clear expectations that it should cease. If they truly did not intend their behavior to have the effect of appearing aggressive, then they should stop what they have been doing and change their behavior. If they do not, then it can be legitimately assumed that they willfully and knowingly acted in such a way as to cause distress or fear in another person, and this clearly would have to be considered to be aggression.

Researchers in the United Kingdom and Australia refer to "bullying," which describes behavior in which one or more people "gang up on" another person or other persons to intimidate, coerce, or directly harm them.[8] In Scandinavia and the German-speaking countries this behavior is referred to as "mobbing."[9] In the United States, researchers have referred to "workplace harassment,"[10] "mistreatment,"[11] and "emotional abuse."[12] Borrowing a term from the clinical literature, Rudy Nydegger has included "passive-aggressive behavior"[13] as a form of workplace aggression.

Most aggression in the workplace is verbal and indirect or passive in form.[14] Although some would question whether this type of behavior would qualify as "violence," few would argue that it is not "aggressive." Typically, in the United States violence and aggression are viewed in relation to views of what constitute "masculine" forms of aggression. These are usually more direct and physical. However, other forms of aggressive behavior may be less direct or physical but nonetheless reflect an aggressive and even violent intention. Many have asserted that men and boys are more aggressive than girls and women at all ages. We counter that this holds only if you define aggression in purely masculine terms. There are other forms of aggressiveness that are more often used by women, and these too are hurtful and damaging. This does not mean that only women use the less direct forms of aggression, for these are found in men and boys too, as we will see later. However, physical violence and aggression are far more likely to be committed by men.

L. Keashly[12] described emotional abuse in the workplace as verbal and nonverbal behaviors that are not explicitly tied to sexual or racial content but are directed to gaining compliance from others. Examples include yelling, screaming, the use of derogatory names, the "silent treatment," withholding information, aggressive eye contact, rumors, explosive outbursts of anger, and ridiculing—especially in front of others. These types of actions as well as other means of intimidating and controlling people are the kinds of behaviors that are often described as bullying or mobbing. Interestingly, according to the Canada Safety Council,[15] while physical violence is often reported from sources outside the organization, psychological violence is more often reported from within the organization. They also report that at least one-fifth of the U.S. workforce had experienced destructive bullying during the past year at work.

Nydegger has described "passive-aggressive"[13] behavior as a form of workplace aggression. He has pointed out that at times subtle and often manipulative behaviors may be disguised and hard to recognize, but they are aggressive nonetheless. This form of aggression is hard to pin down because the perpetrator will invariably deny any aggressive intent. However, when someone consistently does things that are intended to hurt, annoy, bother, or disturb, another person this qualifies as aggression—even though it is passive. Such things as "forgetting" an appointment, not returning phone calls, giving people wrong information, spreading false information or rumors, or other such behaviors are not only aggressive but can cause some real problems. Since the person who perpetrates this type of behavior will usually deny the aggressive intention, how do we know that it is in fact passive aggression? The patterns of behavior will clarify the intention. If the behavior occurs once or twice, it may be a mistake, unintentional, or even misinterpreted. If, on the other hand, this pattern of behavior is consistent and unvarying, and seems to be directed at a specific person or specific persons, then one can assume that the behavior in question is not random and is intended to harm—even if that intent is denied.

Incivility is a milder but still potentially aggressive form of behavior.[5] Rudeness and incivility can also be unintentional, and therefore not really intended to harm others, but when this behavior is inadvertent, it will usually change with feedback or sanctions. When this type of behavior is clearly expressed and seems to be intended to harm or negatively influence others, or if it simply reflects blatant disregard for the feelings and sensibilities of others and does not change with feedback, then it seems clear that this is aggressive and harmful in both intent and effect.

---

### Interview with Dr. Phoebe Morgan, Northern Arizona University

*Question:* Based on your expertise in criminal justice, what steps should employers take to deal with workplace violence?

*Answer:* The key to stopping workplace violence is knowing where, when, and how it is taking place. Employers cannot know how serious the problem is until victims report it. Clinical and organizational research has consistently shown that victims will notify their employers only if they believe that doing so will provide genuine assistance. Thus, my primary recommendation is to create an environment in which workplace violence victims feel truly safe to seek assistance. A truly safe environment begins with the existence of policy and procedures that go beyond merely minimizing the organization's legal liability. Those responsible for handling reports of violence or requests for assistance should be prepared to take all requests for intervention seriously. They should have already on hand a range of practical options for victims to consider. They should be trained to develop and institute practical safety plans. The first step in developing such a plan would require asking victims what actions would make them feel safe and then make a good-faith effort to meet their needs. In sum, without victim cooperation, there is very little employers can do to stop violence in their workplaces. Ending workplace violence begins with ensuring victim safety.

Dr. Phoebe Morgan is an associate professor of criminal Justice at Northern Arizona University. She has been researching and teaching about sexual harassment issues since 1990. In addition, she assists employers with policy reviews, conducts sensitivity training workshops, and provides expert testimony. In 1991, she cofounded the International Consortium against Sexual Harassment (ICASH), and she maintains the ICASH Web site. She recently co-edited *In the Company of Men: Male Dominance and Sexual Harassment* (Northeastern University Press, 2004).

After looking at some of the excellent, well-regarded definitions of violence, our view is consistent with the assertion of Waddington and coauthors[16] that there is no definition of violence that is broad enough to cover the full range of behaviors that comprise it. Thus, rather than being limited by one definition we will focus more on descriptions of phenomena that fall within the broad range of topics of violence and aggression and that inflict many of the same types of harm.

## A MODEL FOR UNDERSTANDING AND MANAGING WORKPLACE VIOLENCE AND MISTREATMENT

If we use a definition that is specific enough to be applicable and testable, then it is not general enough to be applicable to all types of workplace violence. Thus, for example, a good definition of workplace violence probably would not be applicable to incivility or passive-aggressive behavior. On the other hand, if we use a definition that is general enough to apply to all forms of workplace abuse, then it is not specific enough to be helpful in applications or research. In this section we introduce you to a different approach. Rather than trying to create one or many definitions that might appear to work, we decided to offer a model that describes the dimensions of workplace violence that can be applied to any type of this behavior. This approach provides a mechanism for evaluating and understanding *any* form of workplace violence ranging from the most minor to the most horrific.

The dimensions we propose are as follows:

+ Direct—Indirect
+ Active—Passive
+ Intentional—Unintentional
+ Physical—Nonphysical
+ Solitary—Group (perpetrator and victim)
+ Systemic—Nonsystemic
+ High intensity—Low intensity

These dimensions are continuous and not dichotomous. In other words, think of these dimensions as a continuous line with one word at one endpoint and the other word at the other endpoint, as is illustrated below.

Direct ——————————Indirect
Solitary——————————Group

Any behavior can be placed at any point on the continuum, not just at the extremes. This allows our model the flexibility and richness to account for all behavior. We now provide definitions and examples of the dimensions we have identified.

*Direct—Indirect:* Some forms of workplace violence are direct and some are not. For example, hitting or insulting a person is a direct form of abuse.

However, spreading rumors, gossiping, and simply avoiding someone out of spite are more indirect.

*Active—Passive:* Similarly, there are some types of behavior that are very active, and some that are passive. There are some fairly passive forms of behavior that might be very direct, as well as some active types of behavior that are somewhat indirect. For example, suppose a manager said the following to one of her employees: "Gee, this is pretty good. Much better than your usual work." On the surface this appears to be a compliment, but clearly it is a hostile/aggressive message. The behavior itself is direct, although the aggression is passive. Consider another example. An employee actively spreads rumors about a co-worker. In this situation, the effect is not direct, although the aggressive behavior is active.

*Intentional—Unintentional:* When we are talking about aggressive behavior we usually mean something that is intended. However, there are forms of incivility and other forms of mistreatment that are unintentional but still harmful. This includes inconsiderate behavior, neglect, or avoidance that might not even be intended but might still have a negative effect. Thus, this dimension takes into account a range of behavior, from the purely unintentional to the completely intentional. Some might feel that this dimension is best thought of as a dichotomy. From this standpoint, behavior is *either* intentional or it is not. However, as we think about it, it should become clear that sometimes our intentions are difficult to pin down, and sometimes we may not be fully aware of all of our intentions.

*Physical—Nonphysical:* Shooting someone is a very dramatic physical form of aggression. On the other hand, backing someone into a corner and screaming at him or her may not be as physical, but it is still physical. Or, suppose someone "accidentally" bumps into you causing you to spill your coffee. Is this aggressive? Yes! Physical? Yes, but not as physical as the more obvious forms of workplace violence. There are also forms of mistreatment and even aggression that are not physical at all. For example, talking about people behind their back is certainly abusive and might even be aggressive, but it is neither direct nor physical—or at least not very physical. Thus, this dimension clearly covers a broad range of relevant behaviors.

*Solitary—Group:* This dimension can refer to both the victim(s) and the perpetrator(s). It is best to think of it as two dimensions, or perhaps as two subsets of one dimension. We are asserting that the dynamics and impact of abusive behavior can also differ based on the number of people who are involved as perpetrators and as victims.

*Systemic—Nonsystemic:* This dimension refers to the extent to which the abusive behavior in question is part of the fabric or culture of the organization, or whether it is more circumscribed or individual. On one end of this continuum we find systemic behavior that may clearly be part of the organization's policies or processes. For example, suppose that a company has a policy that requires employees to submit to embarrassing interviews periodically to ensure that they are not "morally unfit" to be part of the organization. This type of abusive policy could certainly be considered to be a form of mistreatment, and would also be a formal part of the organization's policy and processes. Thus, it is a systemic form of abuse. Further, elements of an organization's culture might include abusive treatment of new employees as a form of initiation. While this might not be "official," if it is widely accepted and practiced, it would also be systemic.

At the other end of the continuum, we see such behavior as one employee badly treating another employee. It might have nothing to do with the organization at large and would be nonsystemic. In the middle, we find abusive behaviors that are not as widespread but are not as isolated as some of the more obvious examples. Or perhaps we see forms of mistreatment that represent a misuse or misinterpretation of organizational policies. Thus, various forms of abuse or mistreatment can vary, based upon the extent to which the behavior is part of the organization at large.

*High intensity—Low intensity*: Any form of direct or indirect behavior, physical or nonphysical, can also vary based upon the intensity of the behavior. Some acts will be relatively mild and perhaps minimally abusive, and others might be much more severe and highly abusive. By adding this dimension to the model, we can also quantify mistreatment based upon its intensity.

To clarify the application of this model, let's look at some examples and see how they can be analyzed. Suppose that we have a situation in the workplace where one employee becomes angry with a supervisor and purposely pushes her to the ground. Although there are no serious injuries, it is considered to be a significant event and disciplinary measures are taken by the manager of the department. How can our model be used to analyze this situation?

- Direct—Indirect: Very direct. Near the direct pole of the dimension
- Active—Passive: Very active. Near the active pole of the dimension
- Intentional—Unintentional: Clearly intentional, and near that pole of the dimension
- Physical—Nonphysical: Again, obviously physical, and near that pole of the dimension
- Solitary—Group: It is solitary for both the perpetrator and the victim
- Systemic—Nonsystemic: It would appear that there is nothing systemic about this event
- High intensity—Low intensity: While this is a very physical event it is not as intense as a serious assault or homicide, so it would be on the high intensity end, but not at the very end

Another event that is considered to be workplace violence or mistreatment occurs when one employee ignores a new employee and doesn't give him or her any information about how to do the job more easily. Further, this type of behavior is fairly common in the organization, and while it is certainly not company policy, most departments informally treat new employees rather coolly until they have "proven" themselves. How does this type of behavior fit our model?

*Direct—Indirect:* This would depend upon a specific piece of the behavior in question. For example, if the new employee came up to the older employee and asked a question, and the older employee just ignored the question and walked away, this would be very direct. If, on the other hand, the younger employee walked into the room, and the older employee did not greet him or her, but it was not clear whether or not the older employee even saw the new employee, then this might be more indirect.

*Active—Passive:* Once again, this would depend upon the specific behavior in question. If the older employee obviously took steps to avoid or ignore the new employee then it would be active. However, if the older employee really did not do much, either good or bad, relative to the new employee but did not go out of the way to help, then this would be more passive.

*Intentional—Unintentional:* Unless it is believed that the behavior in question was clearly and obviously not intended and was either an oversight or a mistake, then this behavior would be closer to the intentional end of the dimension.

*Physical—Nonphysical:* If the older employee did something obvious like walking around the new employee rather than talking to him or her, then this would be slightly closer to the physical end of the dimension, but most of the behavior in this example would be fairly nonphysical.

*Solitary—Group:* This would depend upon how many young employees and how many older employees were involved. This could range from one to many in both cases.

*Systemic—Nonsystemic:* In this case it would be to some extent toward the systemic side of the dimension. Since this type of behavior is not company policy and is not encouraged or perhaps even known by upper management, then it is not a highly systemic type of behavior. However, since it is a widely practiced type of behavior and is found in more than one setting and practiced by more than one individual, then it is clearly more systemic than not.

*High intensity—Low intensity:* Depending upon the specific behavior in question, this would vary somewhat. It could be very intense, but could be less so as well.

Here is a final example. Jane works for Nerak Corporation, a software development firm. She has worked there for 10 years and until recently has had an excellent work record. In the last six to nine months she has been absent more often, usually on Mondays and Tuesdays. Her productivity has suffered, and she has been less involved with her co-workers, often choosing to eat lunch alone and not joining her co-workers during breaks. Jane has been married for four years to a man with whom she used to be very much in love. They have two children aged three and one (the older being a girl and the younger a boy). Unfortunately, Jane's husband has experienced frequent job changes due to the state of the economy. The stress of parenthood and his feeling that he is not supporting his family have led to increasing use of alcohol and extreme episodes of binge drinking. Although her husband has always had "a bit of a temper" he had never been physically abusive until recently.

In the past year he has been physically abusive to Jane on a number of occasions, following which he has been extremely contrite, promising never to do it again. However, he has repeated the abuse regardless of the promises. Further, the abuse is happening more often and the verbal abuse has been almost a daily event. Jane knows that he has a problem and that he needs help, but he refuses, claiming that he can take care of his problems himself, and he doesn't want to "air the dirty laundry" in front of strangers. Further, Jane fears that if she were to leave him he would simply drink himself into oblivion or even kill himself. She is also afraid that she couldn't support and care for the children on her own. She is too frightened and too embarrassed to talk to anyone on her own, and no one (even among her friends) knows what is happening. Her boss has asked her several times if everything is okay, but she has always just said that taking care of two young children has worn her down, and of course there is an element of truth in that.

This is an example of how domestic violence can impact the work environment even though the actual violence and abuse is occurring elsewhere. Clearly, this situation is affecting Jane, her happiness, her health, and her work. Further, it is harming the organization by decreasing the effectiveness and job satisfaction of an otherwise valuable employee, and it is probably a distraction to other workers as well. Let's see how our model would address these issues, and whether or not it could help us figure out how to manage this situation.

*Direct—Indirect:* Although the violence is direct, the impact on work is not. Thus, from a management situation, you would try to deal with the indirectness by bringing the problem to the forefront. For example, the manager could confront Jane supportively and tell her that if there is something that is bothering her and interfering with her work that he would be happy to help if he could, but that he is concerned about the quality of her work and her productivity, and that he will be monitoring these things. He can then assure her that if there is a problem outside work for which she needs to get help, he will be completely supportive of that, even if she feels that she would rather not discuss it with him.

*Active—Passive:* In this case the abuse is very active, even though it is not apparent at work. Since the effects of the abuse are obvious, the manager should try to deal directly with what is observable. By holding the employee responsible for her performance and offering to support her as needed, the manager will encourage Jane to deal with the active abuse that is occurring.

*Intentional—Unintentional:* The abuse is clearly intentional although the abusive husband would probably try to rationalize his behavior. The manager should treat Jane's behavior as unintentional but encourage her to take control of the situation directly, to exert her will and interest in the situation that is producing the problem.

*Physical—Nonphysical:* Because both the abuse and the results are definitely physical as well as psychological, this would suggest that something needs to be done quickly because there is a risk that something worse will occur, or that at least the same pattern will continue. This is not a situation that should be ignored.

*Solitary—Group:* This directly affects one person and there is one perpetrator. This means that the manager does not need to involve other workers in the problem. If he deals directly with Jane and Jane deals directly with her husband, there is a better chance that this can be dealt with effectively.

*Systemic—Nonsystemic:* This is clearly nonsystemic, and thus the manager does not need to address cultural or work climate issues when addressing the problem.

*High intensity—Low intensity:* This situation is very intense, and thus has a greater potential for escalating and producing bigger problems in the future. Both from the position of the organization and the manager, and from Jane's perspective, this needs to be resolved posthaste.

Once again, it appears that by working through the model step by step, the manager and Jane can both get some ideas as to how to deal with this situation, hopefully to resolve it in as positive a manner as possible. We present additional management strategies for dealing with intimate partner violence as a workplace concern in chapter 6.

As can be seen in the examples given above, the model is useful when applied to specific behaviors. Consequently, with the exception of some extremes, like homicide and serious assault, at one end, and minor events, like pretending not to hear someone, at the other, most behaviors would have a mixture of positions on the various dimensions. However, it seems to us that *any* type of workplace mistreatment ranging from incivility to homicide could be analyzed and understood using this model. It also has implications for establishing effective prevention programs and reacting to workplace violence should it occur, as we discuss in chapter 7.

## RESOURCES

Lim, S., & Cortina, L. (2005). Interpersonal mistreatment in the workplace: The interface and impact of general incivility and sexual harassment. *Journal of Applied Psychology, 90*, 483–496.

Swanberg, J., & Logan, T. (2005). Domestic violence and employment: A qualitative study. *Journal of Occupational Health Psychology, 10*, 3–17.

## Publications of National Institute for Occupational Safety and Health (NIOSH), http://www.niosh.gov

*Violence on the job* (Publication No. 2004–100D).

*Violence: Occupational hazards in hospitals* (Publication No. 2002–101).

*Homicide in U.S. workplaces: A strategy for prevention and research* (Publication No. 92–103).

*Working with stress* (Publication No. 2003–114D).

# CHAPTER 3

# Incidence of Workplace Violence and Impact on Employees and Organizations

If humanity is to evolve beyond the propensity toward violence that now threatens our very survival as a species, then it can only do so by recognizing the extent to which the patriarchal code of honor and shame generates and obligates male violence. If we wish to bring this violence under control, we need to begin by reconstituting what we mean by both masculinity and femininity.

—James Gilligan

The values a man must cherish as his life-breath are: Truth, Righteousness, Peace, Love and Non Violence.

—Sri Sathya Sai Baba

**Questions for Reflection**

+ Do you believe childhood bullies grow up and bully in the workplace too?
+ How do you feel when you are ignored at your job? Have co-workers spread rumors about you? Are your phone calls or e-mails not returned by co-workers when you need information to complete your tasks?
+ Do you believe there are nonviolent types of workplace abuse? Why or why not?
+ Do you have a problem boss? What characterizes a manager or supervisor as "problematic?"

*In 1999, Alan Miller killed two co-workers at their office in Pelham, Alabama, then he killed a third person at a company where he used to work. Also in 1999, investor Mark Barton killed 9 people and wounded 13 at two brokerage firms in Atlanta, and then he killed himself. Prior to the attacks at the brokerage firms, Barton killed his wife and two children.*

When calculating the costs of workplace violence and aggression, as in these two cases, it is difficult to estimate the direct costs, and the indirect and hidden costs will never be fully known. In addition to the financial and other direct costs of violence, there are also many other costs to people, families, organizations, and society. These are harder to estimate, but they are just as real. In this section, we will discuss some of the more obvious costs to individuals and to workplaces. We begin our discussion with an overview of the incidence of workplace violence in a variety of organizational settings.

## INCIDENCE OF WORKPLACE VIOLENCE

Recently, over two million employees reported being attacked at work, resulting in about 13.5 million dollars in medical costs.[1] The National Safe Workplace Institute estimated that in the early 1990s, assaults and murders at work cost the economy over 4.2 billion dollars.[2] In fact, the value of one lost life at work was estimated by the U.S. Department of Labor at seven million dollars.[3] This figure alone suggests that the value of this life will impact the whole economy in many ways that are rarely considered when looking at the costs of workplace violence.

Studies reported by the Teamsters' Union found that up to half a million employees miss 1.8 million days of work each year because of violence at work.[4] This translates into losses in wages of over 55 million dollars. These losses do not include days covered by sick and annual leave. When we include the costs of domestic violence that has spilled over into the workplace, American businesses pay around 3–5 billion dollars annually in medical costs.[5]

One study showed that group harassment and individual bullying of German employees cost employers around 2.5 billion marks per year (this study was concluded before Germany had converted to the euro). In Canada, the British Columbia Workers' Compensation Board reported that lost-wages claims by local hospital workers due to violence had increased by 88 percent in 2001 since 1985.[6] These findings alone, and also taken together with the costs in the United States, suggest that workplace violence is a huge financial burden to companies, governments, and people all over the world.

## WHO ARE THE PERPETRATORS OF WORKPLACE VIOLENCE?

Terms like "going postal" imply that workplace violence is frequently perpetrated by disgruntled or unstable employees. While being murdered by a fellow employee receives a great deal of attention, in reality, it accounts for only 4 percent of workplace homicides.[7] As we discussed in chapter 1, the majority of individuals who commit workplace violence are from outside the organization, and most often the violence occurs during robberies.[8] J. Greenberg and R. Baron presented the following 1997 statistics on the sources of workplace violence:[9]

+ Robberies and other crimes: 81.82%
+ Business disputes: 8.69%
+ Police in the line of duty: 5.59%
+ Personal disputes: 3.9%[9]

The Workplace Violence Headquarters[8] provided these statistics from 2005 on the characteristics of individuals who commit workplace violence:

+ 80% are male over the age of 30.
+ 3% are former employees.
+ 20% are current employees.
+ Two-thirds of physical and verbal attacks come from strangers (e.g., robberies) or customers, especially when the victims are male.
+ Women are more likely to be attacked by someone they know.

The same source also pointed out the differences between those who commit physical violence and those who commit homicide:

| Physical Violence | Homicide |
| --- | --- |
| Customers: 40% | Strangers: 60% |
| Current employees: 26% | Customers: 30% |
| Strangers: 25% | Employees: 7% |
| Domestic spillover: 6% | Domestic spillover: 3% |
| Former employees: 3% | |

Warchol[10] further classified the categories of offenders. Using data from 1992–1996, he pointed out that 82.9 percent of offenders are male and 14.1 percent are female. Racially, 58.4 percent are white, 29.0 percent are African American, and 8.1 percent are individuals of other races. In terms of age, 1.9 percent are under the age of 12, 10 percent are aged 12–17, 6.6 percent are aged 18–20, 29.4 percent are aged 21–29, and 47 percent are over the age of 30. He also reported that in terms of the number of offenders per incident, 84.7 percent of the time there is a solitary perpetrator, 6.2 percent of the time there are two perpetrators, 2.4 percent of the time there are three, and 3.5 percent of the time there are four or more. Clearly gangs and groups can be and are involved in workplace violence and aggression, but it is also clear that by far the largest share of violent acts is committed by individuals acting alone.

R. B. Flannery[11] identified five different types of assailants in the workplace: angry customers, mentally ill persons, batterers in a domestic dispute, criminals, and disgruntled employees. T. Feldman and P. Johnson[12] added disgruntled students/trainees, and abusive supervisors.

As we mentioned previously, the California Occupational Safety and Health Administration (Cal/OSHA)[13] divided workplace violence into three different types based upon the perpetrator of the violence. The types specified by Cal/OSHA are as follows:

+ Type I: Perpetrator with no legitimate connection to the workplace
+ Type II: Fatal or nonfatal injuries to people who provide services to the public
+ Type III: Perpetrator with some employment-related involvement with the workplace

This approach by Cal/OSHA is particularly helpful because it is general enough to cover most if not all incidents, but it also allows for specificity when describing events.

## WHO ARE THE VICTIMS OF WORKPLACE VIOLENCE?

Despite highly publicized cases in which lawyers, brokers, and judges are victims of workplace violence, the real victims are not white-collar workers but those "on the line." Retail workers, convenience store clerks, taxi drivers, and those in similar types of work are far more likely to be victims of workplace violence. Taken from a report from the National Crime Victimization Survey,[14] the following statistics on the victims of workplace violence refer to the period 1993–99:

+ Sex
    + Male: 66.8%
    + Female: 33.2%
+ Race
    + White: 88.6%
    + African American: 8.9%
    + Other racial groups: 2.5%
+ Ethnicity
    + Hispanic: 8.9%
    + Non-Hispanic: 92.1%
+ Age
    + 12–17: 2.4%
    + 18–24: 17.9%
    + 25–34: 32.9%
    + 35–49: 37%
    + 50–59: 7.2%
    + 60–64: 1.5%
    + 65 and over: 1.1%

Employees in retail and service industries are at high risk for workplace violence. Over half of the injury events that occur in work settings are robbery related and approximately 13 percent are fatal. At the highest risk for homicide are men, self-employed persons, and those employed in grocery stores, eating and drinking establishments, gas service stations, taxicab services, and government services, including law enforcement. Unlike homicides, the majority of nonfatal events leading to lost work time affect women, primarily those in health care or other service sector work. The assault rates for residential, nursing home, and personal care workers are more than 10 times greater than those for workers in private, non-health care industries.[15]

E. Q. Bulatao and G. R. VandenBos[16] noted that taxi drivers were at the highest risk for homicides at work, but they also confirmed that nonfatal assaults were more common in service and retail businesses. In the service sector they too found that most assaults were in health care, with 27 percent of the violent events occurring in nursing homes, 13 percent in social services, and 11 percent in hospitals.

Another special case of workplace violence victims involves government workers.[16] Government employees make up 18 percent of the U.S. workforce but account for 30 percent of the victims of workplace violence. The types of public employees who are at risk other than public safety (police and fire) employees include, for example, the following : health care workers, correctional officials, social service workers, teachers, municipal housing inspectors, and public works employees.[17] These occupations put them in contact with people who may be at high risk for committing workplace violence and makes them more likely to be victimized.

Warchol[10] presented summary data on the victims of workplace violence. The two types of employees that are most likely to be victims of workplace violence (in terms of total numbers of events), are retail sales workers (330,000 events) and police officers (234,200 events). Warchol's data summarized the rates for various occupational groups, listed according to the number of events per 1,000 workers annually. These rates are as follows:

- Police: 306
- Private security guards: 218
- Taxi drivers: 184 (although they have the highest rate of workplace homicide)
- Prison guards: 117
- Bartenders: 91
- Mental health professionals: 80
- Gas station attendants: 79
- Convenience/liquor store clerks: 68
- Mental health custodial workers: 63
- Junior high/middle school teachers: 57
- Bus drivers: 45
- Special education teachers: 41

+ High school teachers: 16
+ College teachers: 3

Warchol[10] also reported the following areas in which workplace violence is likely to occur:

+ Cities: 56.5%
+ Suburbs: 14.6%
+ Rural communities: 10.8%
+ More than one of the above: 17.7%
+ Unsure: 0.4%

Workplace violence is found to differ from non-workplace violence according to the time at which the violent acts are committed, the age of the victims, the degree of victim injury, and whether or not the workplace is in a medical setting. The differences between workplace and non-workplace violence are best explained by the movement of people in and out of the workplace who bring societal violence with them. rather than by category or type of workplace violence.[18] Thus, the best way to understand *most* workplace violence is to realize that it is very frequently due to the prevalence of the societal violence found in the workplace's environment, and that workplace violence is often a variant of this societal violence that is brought into the workplace.

Clearly there are many, varied types of jobs that put employees at some degree of risk. We will discuss specific risk factors and the ways to minimize them in chapter 4.

## IMPACT ON INDIVIDUALS

There is a substantial potential for financial, physical, and psychological harm to result from workplace violence.[19] In the aftermath of violence, the survivors who were injured, those who may have been targeted but were missed or spared, those who witnessed the events, co-workers, family, friends, and other people in the organization may all experience emotionally devastating consequences. For the victims and their co-workers it is clear that the work environment has become a dangerous place and is no longer a safe haven.[20]

When determining the types of effects that workplace violence will have on people, a number of elements should be considered: the age of the victim, the amount of family support available, the victim's experience in similar situations, whether the victim has survived other stressful situations and how he or she has dealt with them, and the victim's perceptions of the incident. It should also be noted that a person's typical coping mechanisms will usually be inadequate for dealing with the aftermath of workplace violence.

Following a traumatic violent event, victims are susceptible to the development of post-traumatic stress disorder (PTSD) and other psychological problems.[21] Immediately following workplace violence, people usually experience shock, a sense of disbelief, and physical and psychological numbing. According to T. Barnett-Queen and L. H. Bergman,[22] in the hours and days following a traumatic event like workplace violence, three different types of consequences are common among most victims:

+ Re-experiencing consequences—e.g., obsessive thinking, dreaming, flashbacks, etc.
+ Withdrawal consequences—social and physical withdrawal, absenteeism, voluntary turnover, etc.
+ Other consequences—e.g., anger, irritability, sleep problems, problems concentrating, and an exaggerated startle response

Furthermore, there is always a concern about recurrence, and this is an almost universal concern among victims and their co-workers, families, and friends. In fact, the more meaningless and arbitrary the incident, the more vulnerable and unsafe the survivors are likely to feel.[23] Barnett-Queen and Bergman[22] reported that many survivors of workplace violence indicate they are very tired, have difficulty concentrating, and have problems remembering important information. We should also point out that whenever an incident of workplace violence occurs, there is an impact not only on those directly involved but also on many others as well. These others include people who have no connection with the work environment in which the violence occurred but who have heard about it through the media and other sources. People who will never be directly evaluated as affected by the event will vicariously experience some of the fears and concerns that would be expected of the employees at the site of the violence. Simply reading about, hearing about, or learning about violence probably has an impact on many people.

In addition to physical injuries, violent, abusive, or threatening events at work often result in serious and disabling psychological damage. As mentioned above, victims are at high risk for PTSD, and while psychological trauma is a frequent result of workplace violence we know far less about it than we know about the physical harm that might occur. Some of the psychological/emotional problems that may result from workplace violence include self-doubt, depression, fear, loss of sleep, irritability, disturbed relationships with family, friends, and co-workers, decreased ability to function normally at work, and increased absenteeism. Further, employees often blame themselves when they are impaired by an assault, and too frequently management encourages this blame.[22]

Employees whose job experience has been impacted by interpersonal aggression will very probably experience greater fear and a negative mood at work.[23] This in turn is likely to reduce job satisfaction.[24] This finding is important because we also know that job satisfaction is a good predictor of voluntary turnover: the lower the job satisfaction, the higher the turnover.[25] It has also been demonstrated that there is a direct relationship between job satisfaction and organizational citizenship (doing more for the organization than is required) and a direct relationship between job satisfaction and job performance.[26] It is obvious that not only does workplace violence have a significant and substantial impact on victims and others; it also has a direct impact on the functioning of the organization. Management should certainly take heed when it realizes the direct and indirect costs of workplace violence to the organization.

As important as the impact of workplace violence is for the organization, its employees, and many others as well, many people feel that the long-term effects of such violence can be minimized or even prevented. The overall goals for victims of workplace violence in dealing with their emotional reactions are as follows:

+ Reduction of the disturbing symptoms
+ Enhancement of emotional expression
+ Assimilation of the traumatic event[27]

The National Center for Victims of Crime[19] pointed out that the process of resolution for victims of workplace violence can be facilitated by family and friends who acknowledge the trauma, allow the individual to talk about it, and accept the uneven road to resolution. The center also pointed out that some people will need more than simple debriefing and support from family. It is rare that these complex problems are dealt with effectively in the short term; there is increasing evidence that victims and witnesses of violent incidents need long-term treatment to fully overcome the problems.[23] Suffice it to say that some will rebound fairly quickly with minimal intervention, some will need a little more in the form of short-term treatment, and others will need longer, more intensive treatment to fully recover. Dealing with the aftereffects of violence means taking care of individual *and* organizational needs.

## RESOURCES

Barling, J., Bluen, S., & Fain, R. (1987). Psychological functioning following an acute disaster. *Journal of Applied Psychology, 72*, 683–690.

Schat, A., & Kelloway, E. (2000). Effects of perceived control on the outcomes of workplace aggression and violence. *Journal of Occupational Health Psychology, 5*, 386–402.

VandenBos, G., & Bulatao, E. (Eds.). (1996). *Violence on the job: Identifying risks and developing solutions.* Washington, DC: American Psychological Association.

## Publications of U.S. Department of Labor, Occupational Safety and Health Administration (OSHA), http://www.osha.gov

*OSHA guidelines for preventing workplace violence for health care and social service workers* (2004).

*Risk factors and protective measures for taxi and livery drivers* (2000).

*Recommendations for workplace violence prevention in late-nite retail establishments* (OSHA National News Release, 1998).

# CHAPTER 4

# Factors Contributing to Workplace Violence

The right things to do are those that keep our violence in abeyance; the wrong things are those that bring it to the fore.

—Robert J. Sawyer

It is clear that the way to heal society of its violence … and lack of love is to replace the pyramid of domination with the circle of equality and respect.

—Manitonquat

All violence, all that is dreary and repels, is not power, but the absence of power.

—Ralph Waldo Emerson

There is no way to peace. Peace is the way.

—A. J. Muste

### Questions for Reflection

+ Can you "spot" a potential violent co-worker? Why or why not?
+ If you were to participate in a company-sponsored training program on workplace violence, what would you like to know about individuals who are violent in the workplace?
+ Think of some television programs you often watch. Do they contain violence? Is the violence romanticized or glorified? Have you ever considered voicing your opinions about the violence portrayed on television?

+ Why do you believe workplace violence is an uncomfortable topic to discuss?
+ Have you received training from your employer about workplace violence? Would you feel comfortable discussing this issue with your supervisor? Why or why not?

---

*November 2, 1999: Byran Uyesugi, a repair person for Xerox in Honolulu, killed seven co-workers before fleeing in a company van. He surrendered after a five-hour standoff with police.*

*August 5, 1999: Alan Eugene Miller, an employee of a heating and air conditioning company, shot two co-workers to death in Pelham, Alabama. He then killed a third person at a business where he had once worked.*

*March 6, 1998: A former accountant for the Connecticut Lottery Corporation, Matthew Beck, 35, fatally shot four senior executives of the lottery and then killed himself.*

*December 18, 1997: Arturo Reyes Torres, 43, killed four former co-workers at a maintenance yard in Orange, California, and was shot to death by police.*

*September 15, 1997: Fired assembly line worker Arthur H. Wise, 43, opened fire at an Aiken, South Carolina, parts plant, killing four people and wounding three others.*

Do you believe these incidents share some commonalities with regard to the factors contributing to workplace violence? According to K. T. Liou,[1] there are three interrelated sources of workplace violence or factors contributing to it: personal causes; work and organizational factors; and societal issues. D. Chappell and V. DeMartino[2] also listed a number of factors contributing to workplace violence, including the following: individual behavior; the work environment; the conditions of work; the ways in which co-workers interact; the ways in which customers or clients interact with workers; and the interactions between managers and workers. Clearly, there are various factors that contribute to workplace violence.

S. C. Douglas and M. J. Martinko[3] aptly predicted "that the interaction of individual and situational factors will provide the best explanation for the variability in the incidence of workplace aggression." We will now examine some of the factors that have been determined to be related to the incidence of workplace violence and/or aggression.

## PERSONAL AND PSYCHOLOGICAL FACTORS

What are the kinds of individual characteristics that might lead employees to behave violently or aggressively at work? Interestingly, if we ask those who have committed violent or aggressive acts why they have done so, they rarely point to some characteristic or trait they possess to explain their actions.

Typically, they will say that someone did something to them that justified the aggressive response.[4] That is, they will often externalize the responsibility for their act, and feel that it was not their fault because someone else "drove" them to do what they did. In fact, they frequently imply that any reasonable person would have done the same thing. Of course, this explanation is rarely satisfactory to anyone besides the perpetrator.

Liou[1] summarized much of the research evidence by pointing out the following personal characteristics that have been associated with workplace aggression: personal values; job attitudes and behaviors; socialization in the society; personality and motivation; personal habits and problems; perceived anger and stress; and negative personal experiences. Douglas and Martinko[3] included trait anger, attribution style, negative affectivity, attitudes toward revenge, self-control, and previous exposure to aggressive cultures. These factors taken together accounted for 62 percent of the variance in predicting workplace aggression. Clearly, there are some personal characteristics that may not directly *cause* violence or aggression but are predisposing factors that obviously play some type of role.

R. A. Baron and D. R. Richardson[5] found that individuals with low self-control manifest a fairly stable tendency (predisposition) to react with offense to provocations that are relatively small. Similarly, Douglas and Martinko[3] examined trait anger (i.e., disposition to experience chronic feelings of anger over time and across situations) and found this to be a stable disposition that is consistent over time and context and might range from mild annoyance to rage. Of importance here is also the fact that trait anger is one of the factors that statistically predicts workplace violence when taken into account with other relevant variables.

One variable that has been somewhat controversial in the literature is the Type A personality.[6] Originally, this was said to be related to early-onset cardiovascular disease, although with subsequent research this finding has been declared to be oversimplified. However, with respect to workplace violence it has been found that Type A people are more aggressive than others, elicit more aggression from others, and are more easily frustrated, which can also lead to higher levels of aggression.[7]

Another variable that has been related to workplace violence and aggression is self-monitoring. This variable has to do with the extent to which people are aware of their own behavior and are sensitive to its impact on others. High self-monitors are exceedingly aware of their own behavior and its impact on others, and thus their behavior shows high levels of contextual relevance. Thus, their behavior will change in order to adapt to different situations. Low self-monitors, on the other hand, are not nearly as aware of the effects of their behavior on others, nor do they seem to be as aware of their own behavior. Thus, their behavior is much more stable across situations and does not adapt as readily to changing situations.

Rudy Nydegger[8] pointed out that low self-monitoring could lead to aggression; if individuals are unaware of the effect of their behavior on others, they might be obstructionist or inconsiderate and not even be aware of it. Thus, their behavior might not itself be aggressive, but it could lead to aggressive behavior in others. Low self-monitoring people might also have a hostile attributional bias since others might really be more hostile to them, and this might lead to more aggressive behavior as well.[9] Thus, in rather indirect ways, self-monitoring might be related to workplace violence and aggression.

Another psychological variable that has been related to workplace violence and aggression is negative affectivity. This refers to an individual's prevailing mood. If someone is frequently in a bad mood, this is an example of negative affectivity. Several researchers have suggested that negative affectivity is related to interpersonal conflict and to aggressive behavior.[10] Others have asserted that a negative affective state can lead to people behaving more aggressively and eliciting more aggressive behavior from others. In addition, individuals with negative affectivity frequently tend to externalize and blame others, which may also lead to more aggression.[11] However, it should also be noted that in their research, Douglas and Martinko[3] did not find that negative affectivity was related to workplace aggression. Thus, while it seems to make sense that people in a consistently bad mood might be more likely to behave aggressively and to possibly evoke aggressive behavior from others, it may not be as simple as that.

Finally, another psychological factor related to workplace violence is domestic violence, also referred to as intimate partner violence. A person who is a victim of domestic violence has a higher risk of also being a victim of violence in the workplace. The reason for this is that domestic violence too often spills over into the work environment. Thus, the victim of violence at home is now a victim of violence at work, although the perpetrator is usually the same person in both settings.[12] We will discuss domestic violence as a workplace concern in chapter 6.

## BEHAVIORAL RISK FACTORS

In addition to psychological and personal factors, some behavioral indicators are also related to violence and aggression at work. The two most obvious behavioral indicators are a history of aggressive acting out and substance abuse. L. Greenberg and J. Barling[13] found that a history of aggression and alcohol consumption predicted employee aggression toward co-workers. Another behavioral factor is the desire to seek revenge. This is what N. Stuckles and R. Goranson refer to as the "proclivity to inflict damage, injury or punishment in return for an injury, insult, or perceived harm.[14] Douglas and Martinko[3] found that this desire to seek revenge was directly related to workplace aggression. Thus, a person who is predisposed to seek revenge for real or imagined harm or slights may well be capable of violence or aggression at work or elsewhere.[15]

It has been demonstrated that if individuals are behaviorally or psychologically frustrated (prevented from achieving a goal) they are at higher risk of being aggressive.[16] Nydegger[8] suggested this can happen in the workplace because the work environment might well present difficult and frustrating situations that might lead to aggression. Behaviorally, then, seeing and/or experiencing frustration at work, or carrying frustration from outside into the work environment, could certainly create situations resulting in violence or aggression.

It is not uncommon for employees to feel that they are being treated unfairly. Interestingly, it is not so much the fact of being treated unfairly as the employee's *perception* of being treated unfairly that can cause problems. Employees who feel that they are being treated unfairly are at higher risk of engaging in violence and aggression, and some employees will even aggress against the organization by theft or vandalism to "get even" for perceived unfairness.[17]

Another behavioral indicator of potential risk for violence or aggression is the use of threats. Of course, most people who threaten do not follow through, but it is difficult to determine who will actually act on threats and who will not. Much of the research that has been done on the relationship between threats and violence has been done on people with serious mental illnesses.[18] Most people who threaten others may not behave violently or aggressively, but since we cannot easily determine who is serious and who is not, the best advice to most organizations is to take threats seriously. We would also point out that the act of making threats to others is an aggressive act itself, and deserves to be treated seriously.

How then can we predict what kinds of behaviors are indicative of a person who is prone to violence? First, when we look at the lists of warning signs, the more signs a person manifests, the higher the risk. Second, the more recent the observed signs, the higher the risk. According to research, the following are warning signs that should lead an employer or supervisor to take them seriously and probably intervene:[19]

- Personal changes of any kind
- Chemical dependency
- Severe depression
- Romantic obsession that is ignored or rejected
- Constant blaming of others
- High level of frustration with work or personal issues
- Fascination with weapons, violence, or terrorism
- Inability to accept criticism
- Feelings of injustice or unfairness
- Social isolation or low self-esteem

+ Continuing disputes with co-workers or family
+ Controlling and demanding presence

L. H. Pastor[20] identified a similar list of warning signs. He asked managers to answer the following questions regarding their employees:

+ Have they made threats?
+ Do they have a history of violence?
+ Do they have paramilitary interests?
+ Do they have access to weapons?
+ Do they act paranoid?
+ Do they have a history of substance abuse?
+ Do they believe there is no future or no apparent alternative to violence?

The California Occupational Safety and Health Administration (Cal/OSHA) also suggested behavioral and attitudinal indicators of potential problem behaviors:[21]

+ Being upset over recent events
+ Exhibiting recent major changes in behavior, demeanor, or appearance
+ Withdrawing from normal activities, family, friends, and/or co-workers
+ Intimidating, verbally abusing, harassing, or mistreating others
+ Challenging or resisting authority for unclear or inappropriate reasons
+ Blaming others for problems in life/work, being suspicious, holding grudges
+ Using/abusing alcohol and/or recreational drugs
+ Giving unwelcome, obsessive romantic attention
+ Stalking
+ Making threatening references to other incidents of violence
+ Making threats to harm oneself, others, or property
+ Having weapons or being fascinated with weapons
+ Having a known history of violence
+ Communicating specific proposed acts of disruption or violence

In terms of organizational outcomes, some of the consequences of what C. Meyhew and D. Chappell[22] called "internal violence" include the following:

+ Downsizing
+ Unfair treatment
+ Jobs moving offshore
+ Rapid change
+ Stress
+ Changes in workload and pace of work
+ Career concerns
+ Changes in work scheduling
+ Role stresses
+ Effects on interpersonal relationships
+ Job content and control issues
+ Wage freezes

+ Cost cutting and budgetary constraints
+ Autocratic management practices
+ Changes in environmental conditions

   Employees who display behavioral indicators may not be violent or aggressive at all, but they do bear observation and/or counseling.[23] Often when people are troubled and seem to be "falling apart," others avoid them, talk about them, and demean them. A kind or sympathetic word or even sincere concern from a co-worker or supervisor might be the one thing that turns the situation around and actually *reduces* the risk of violence.[8]

## ORGANIZATIONAL FACTORS RELATED TO VIOLENCE AND AGGRESSION

   Very often when violence occurs in the workplace it is easiest to lay all the blame on the perpetrator without examining some of the contextual factors that might play a contributing role. Thus, we frequently miss factors that might be related to workplace violence or aggression and that could be dealt with before they contribute to a problem. Let us point out, however, that making this point in no way implies that people are not responsible for their own behavior. Rather, if we really want to understand and minimize workplace violence and aggression, we must understand as many of the contributing factors as we can, and deal with them in such a way as to make the work environment safer. Clearly, if it were as simple as saying that certain workplace factors "cause" violence or aggression, then everyone in the situation would be committing violent and aggressive acts, and this is never the case. Thus, it cannot *only* be situational factors that are responsible for violence and aggression, but to ignore these factors is to invite trouble. There will certainly be some employees who might not be aggressive *except* in the particular circumstances found in a specific organization at a specific time.

   Workplace stress certainly increases the probability that violence and/or aggression will emerge in a given setting. Even environmental conditions like noise, heat, and humidity can create stress that might lead to increases in aggression. Given that stress can be and often is related to aggression in the workplace, we should look for the types of organizational situations that lead to stress, and see what the effects might be. Whenever there is change, there is stress, and extreme forms of change are the most stressful. In fact, as Rudy Nydegger[8] pointed out, even good change leads to stress, and when evaluating a setting for its "stress potential" we must look at all of the changes that are taking place, both good and bad. However, as one might expect, negative changes are most frequently associated with an increased risk of violence or aggression.

   We only need to look at our homes and workplaces to realize that rapid social and technological change has created highly stressful lifestyles for many people. Rapidly accumulating evidence demonstrates that with increasing stress we also find an increase in general psychological tension and a dramatic rise in such stress-related diseases as hypertension and coronary disease.[24] In fact, people in jobs that require interpersonal contact typically show increased pulse rates, higher diastolic blood pressure, and, among smokers, an increase in smoking behavior, which carries its own health risks.[25]

B. Sharif[26] pointed out some of the sources of stress that are found in the workplace:

+ Over- and underwork
+ Quantitative work overload (especially during economically depressed times when people often do double their usual amount of work)
+ Qualitative overload (where people may not have the knowledge, skills, or abilities to actually perform their jobs)
+ Underutilization of workers (where people are overskilled or overqualified for their jobs)
+ Lack of involvement with the decision making that affects one's work
+ Job insecurity and job loss
+ Cutbacks and layoffs
+ Interpersonal conflicts

K. R. Pelletier[27] suggested that stress-related disorders often result from environmental factors like crowded work areas, noise, inadequate lighting, and poor ventilation. He also reported that psychological factors like aggressive or absent communication with management, rush deadlines, and job insecurity all create stress that might be related to workplace violence and aggression.

The effects of stress are persistent and pervasive. This means that the effects of even small stresses do not go away quickly and they are not situation specific, as stress experienced in one setting will carry over into other situations. Thus, when we look for the effects of stress on workplace violence and aggression we may miss some of the most important stressors if we ignore the small, persistent, and uncontrollable annoyances that can build up and create severe problems.

Recognizing the early signs of mismanagement of stress allows employers to intervene to prevent stress from leading to or contributing to workplace violence and aggression.[28] Obviously, we will never (nor should we even try to) eliminate all stress from our lives or from our work environments. Stress is simply inevitable. However, we do not have to be fatalistic and pessimistic about it. We can certainly agree that stress can have many negative effects on people and on the work environment. In fact, it seems clear that severe or even minor stressors that are unrelenting can produce aggressive and even violent behavior in people. If organizations are serious about reducing the threat of workplace violence and aggression, they should pay attention to controllable stress at work and take steps to minimize its impact.

Whenever an organization or its members are faced with "critical incidents," we can expect increased stress. This stress will increase the likelihood of violence and aggression. Such critical incidents include assaults, robberies, hate crimes, domestic violence, explosions in the workplace, fire, harassment, industrial accidents, death or extended illness of workers or colleagues, hostile terminations, layoffs and downsizing, natural disasters, stalking of an employee, sudden death or injury of workers or colleagues, and threats of violence. Liou mentioned the following as work and organizational factors that have been specifically linked to workplace violence:[1]

+ Organizational structure
+ Administrative processes
+ Supervisory styles
+ Nature of job and task
+ Managerial policies
+ Organizational culture and environment
+ Employee perspective on the organization and its processes
+ Employee reactions to new management philosophy and strategy of downsizing

The National Institution for Occupational Safety and Health (NIOSH)[29] identified additional factors in the workplace that are associated with increased risks of violence and aggression:

+ Exchange of money
+ Contact with the public
+ Delivery of passengers, goods, or services
+ Having a mobile workplace (e.g., taxicab or police cruiser)
+ Working with unstable or volatile persons in health care, social service, or criminal justice setting
+ Working alone or in small numbers
+ Working late at night or during early morning hours
+ Working in high-crime areas
+ Guarding valuable property or possessions
+ Working in community-based settings

Health24.com[30] asked the interesting question: "Are you a problem boss?" This Web site pointed out that if you are a boss who uses aggressive and passive-aggressive strategies in dealing with employees, you may see some of the following results:

+ High turnover
+ Negative assessment from employees (positive to your face, but negative to others)
+ Factions among the staff (we-they; in-group/out-group, etc.)
+ Work-to-rule ("Why should I do that? It's not my job.")
+ Decreased productivity
+ Frequent complaints
+ Increased use of sick time

- Sudden silence when you enter a room
- Unpleasant atmosphere at work
- Little cooperation or teamwork
- Nervous employees
- Frequent misinterpretations of instructions
- Disrespectful behavior

Obviously, if the boss isn't the problem, then he or she needs to look elsewhere, but very often supervisors tend to "blame downward." Too often, bosses see the problems in their subordinates. Of course, they do not always make these assumptions, but we think that in many situations, management or organizational factors may be a good place to start looking for problems and solutions.

Numerous studies and articles have looked at violence and aggression or, as TTG Consultants[31] referred to it, "workplace terrorism." TTG Consultants listed organizational factors such as downsizing, unfair treatment, manufacturing moving offshore, rapid and unexpected change, and workplace stress as being related to "terrorism" in the workplace. Similarly, the Teamsters[32] pointed out the following factors contributing to the violence and aggression that impacts employees: low staffing levels, working alone, working with money, working in organizations where there are long waits for customers, and a lack of support services for employees. In addition, J. Brockner and coauthors[33] pointed out that organizational events or situations that create hostility can and do lead to workplace problems of violence and aggression. Thus, layoffs, downsizing, and wage freezes may not "cause" violence, but they often lead to increased feelings of hostility, which may in turn lead to violence and aggression. One interesting observation comes from R. Baron and J. Neumann,[34] who pointed out that in some organizations the normative structure of the group or organization itself may actually support or lead to aggression or violence. In other organizations, the violation of certain norms may result in violence or aggression.

If employees tend to attribute negative workplace outcomes to other people or to their employers, and believe that these outcomes are controllable, then workplace aggression will be more frequent than if the same employees interpret events as unintentional and uncontrollable. Thus, it is not just the presence of organizational factors but, rather, how employees perceive them, and whether or not they feel that people mean to harm them or could have prevented harm that actually leads to aggression. Similarly, D. P. Skarlicki and R. Folger[35] pointed out that employees are less likely to retaliate against their employers when they perceive procedures to be fair. These findings remind us of what psychologists have known for a very long time: it is not exactly the situation that people respond to but their *perception* of the situation that determines how they act.

Other researchers have attempted to link workplace violence and aggression to factors like leadership style in organizations, but this is not as easy to demonstrate. One study, by W. Hepworth and A. Towler,[36] did demonstrate that charismatic leadership is negatively correlated with workplace aggression. Although this was statistically significant, it explained only 3 percent of the variance in workplace aggression, and was clearly not a very robust predictor. Thus, it is not likely that one could take a very volatile situation or potentially aggressive employees and turn the situation around simply by implementing a specific style of leadership. Not that this would be a bad thing to do, but by itself it would not be likely to erase all of the other risk factors.

It is vitally important that when dealing with organizational factors related to violence and aggression, we also keep in mind cultural factors that contribute to or support actors related to the continuance of aggression. Employees and supervisors must believe that if things are ever going to get better they have to deal with things as they happen. In addition, managers and employers must communicate in the strongest possible terms that problems have to be reported and will be dealt with fairly and consistently. If employees do not believe that anyone cares, or worse, that they will be punished for pointing out or reporting aggression when it occurs, then it will not only continue but it will flourish.

## SOCIAL AND CULTURAL FACTORS RELATED TO WORKPLACE VIOLENCE AND AGGRESSION

There is certainly little question that we live in a society fraught with violence and aggression. Some feel strongly that one of the factors related to aggression in the workplace is societal violence, which intrudes into organizations from the outside. Liou[1] listed a number of societal factors that are thought to be related to workplace violence:

+ Tradition and culture
+ Public attitudes
+ Family composition
+ Social values
+ Economic conditions
+ Political philosophy
+ Public policies
+ Technological development
+ Mass media
+ Influence of society on employee perceptions
+ Interaction of social issues and the modern organization
+ Increasing public concern about the government

According to the American Federation of State, County, and Municipal Employees (AFSCME),[37] we live in a more violent society than ever, with more guns accessible than ever, and more people willing to solve their problems with violence. Naturally, they assert, more violence will spill over into the workplace if there is more violence outside it. The Teamsters[32] reported that much of the violence in the workplace stems from the violent environment outside. They further suggested that as society becomes more violent it also becomes more dangerous to employees. The fact that many organizations are housed in violent neighborhoods where weapons are readily available also increases the risks for violence and aggression.

One further issue is that many patients with severe mental illnesses are discharged early from hospitals without adequate services to maintain them on the "outside," and these patients can also be a threat to employees. Similarly, criminals who are released early, who are not followed adequately, or who are hospitalized rather than incarcerated can create problems for employees. This theme is also addressed by AFSCME,[37] which pointed out that deinstitutionalization has put people on the streets who should be institutionalized. Health care and social service workers, particularly, have to deal with patients who may be difficult or dangerous. Often the agencies or institutions that have to deal with these patients are chronically understaffed.

## THE MEDIA AND WORKPLACE VIOLENCE

There is one social/cultural factor that bears discussion on its own, and that is the effect of the media on violent and aggressive behavior. This is an issue that has generated considerable controversy, but it certainly deserves serious discussion as a factor that might be related to workplace violence and aggression.

The first systematic study of this phenomenon was by A. Bandura and others, who published their results in 1961.[38] These authors reported that children were more aggressive after watching an adult role model and a cartoon character behaving aggressively. This study stimulated considerable discussion among researchers and educators, but it did not dramatically alter television and movie programming, nor did it reduce the production of aggressive toys. Throughout the years, many researchers have continued to point out that exposure to media violence significantly enhances a viewer's aggressive behavior. Huesmann and coauthors reported[39] that there are numerous experimental studies, many observational studies, and even a few longitudinal studies all indicating that exposure to dramatic violence on television and in the movies is related to violent behavior. Huesmann and coauthors[39] also pointed out that childhood exposure to media violence predicts violent behavior in young adults of both sexes. It is also reported that identification with aggressive television characters and the perceived realism of television violence also predicts later aggression. More impressively, the authors found that these effects persist even when the effects of socioeconomic status, intellectual ability, and a variety of parenting factors are controlled. They also reported in a 15-year follow-up study of 329 youths that exposure to television violence between the ages of 6 and 9 predicted direct aggressiveness for male and female adolescents, and also predicted indirect aggression for female adolescents.

J. Cantor[40] demonstrated that the viewing of media violence is consistently associated with higher levels of antisocial behavior ranging from trivial to serious and covering everything in between. In another study, J. Johnson and others[41] reported, television viewing and aggressive behavior were assessed over a 17-year period in a group of 707 male and female participants. They found a clear and positive relationship between the amounts of time spent watching television during adolescence and early adulthood and the likelihood of subsequent aggressive acts against other people. This relationship was still significant when the effects of previous aggressive behavior, childhood neglect, family income, neighborhood violence, parental education, and psychiatric disorders were statistically controlled.

Others have suggested that the relationship between exposure to violence in the media and subsequent violent or aggressive behavior is not quite so simple. In fact, it is clear that not all children or adolescents who are exposed to violent media become violent people. There is obviously more to consider here. Slater and others[42] found that aggressive youth actively seek out media violence, and also that media violence predicts violent behavior in youth. They suggested that this interaction causes a "downward spiral," which leads to higher levels of violence among susceptible youth. What this suggests is that some youth are more affected by media violence than others, and unfortunately, this group also more actively seeks out stimulation from violent media. In a subsequent study, Slater and others[42] reported, the effect of media violence leading to aggressive behavior in youth was found to be more robust among students who reported feelings of alienation from school and during times of increased peer victimization. In the aftermath of tragedies such as Columbine, these findings are very chilling. One might argue that the Columbine tragedy occurred in a school and not a workplace. However, the school *is* the workplace for all of the teachers and school employees, and schools are one of the work environments where violence can be a real problem.

The media industry, as one might expect, also weighs in against the findings suggesting that media violence leads to aggressive behavior. Leonard Goldenson of ABC states that "many Americans are reluctant to accept the images reflected by the mirror we have held up to our society."[43] Similarly, Julian Goodman of NBC says that "The medium is being blamed for the message."[43]

Consistently, the media industry claims that it is simply presenting images of society as it exists, and providing people with "what they want to see."

Michael Medved[44] discussed some of the media industry's "lies" and pointed out how distorted is the claim that television is only reflecting society. He pointed out that about 350 characters appear on television each night in prime time and about seven are murdered each night. If this same rate actually existed in society, then everyone in the United States would be killed in 50 days. M. B. Oliver[45] studied "reality-based" police shows on television and reported some interesting findings. First, in "real life" about 87 percent of all crimes are nonviolent, whereas only 13 percent of crimes on "reality" television are nonviolent. Further, only 0.2 percent of crimes reported by the FBI are murders, whereas about 50 percent of the crimes shown on reality-based television shows are murders. The facts seem clear that although it is not a simple relationship, exposing children and youth to violent media puts them at higher risk for committing violent acts later. Further, the more violence that youngsters are exposed to, the more likely they are to act violently. It is a complex issue, but this fact does not negate the general and consistent findings that violent media can have a negative impact on the people who watch. Parents should monitor the types and amounts of violence to which their children are exposed. To pretend that we can protect our children from violence in the media or in real life is dangerously shortsighted. However, to assume that there is nothing that we can do about it is equally dangerous.

According to Huesmann and colleagues,[39] "Most researchers of aggression agree that severe aggressive and violent behavior seldom occurs unless there is a convergence of multiple predisposing and precipitating factors such as neurophysiological abnormalities, poor child rearing, socioeconomic deprivation, poor peer relations, attitudes and beliefs supporting aggression, drug and alcohol abuse, frustration and provocation, and other factors." It is apparent that there are social factors that are related to the appearance of violence and aggression in general and also in organizational settings. Complex behavior has multiple and complex determinants, and, as we shall see, these require complex and multifaceted interventions to control or eliminate them.

## RESOURCES

Baron, S. (2001). *Violence in the workplace: A prevention and management guide for businesses.* New York: Pathfinder.

Bowie, V., Fisher, B., & Cooper, C. (Eds.). (2005). *Workplace violence: Issues, trends, strategies.* New York: Willan.

Nydegger, R. (2000). Violence, aggression and passive-aggression in the workplace. *Management Development Forum, 3*, 89–96.

VandenBos, G., & Bulatao, E. (Eds.). (1996). *Violence on the job: Identifying risks and developing solutions.* Washington, DC: American Psychological Association.

## Associations Dealing with Workplace Stress

Centre for Stress Management
http://www.managingstress.com

International Stress Management Association
PO Box 348
Waltham Cross EN8 8ZL, UK

# CHAPTER 5

# Workplace Sexual Harassment

I have a dream that my four little children will one day live in a nation where they will not be judged by the color of their skin but by the content of their character.

—Martin Luther King, Jr.

In the end antiblack, antifemale, and all forms of discrimination are equivalent to the same thing—antihumanism.

—Shirley Chisholm

How I wish we lived in a time when laws were not necessary to safeguard us from discrimination.

—Barbra Streisand

I believe that those who promote discrimination on the basis of sexual orientation or any other grounds are gravely mistaken about the values that make our nation strong. I will continue to move my administration in the direction of compassion.

—Bill Clinton

## Questions for Reflection

- Do you believe you have experienced discrimination at your job? In your educational career? Why or why not?
- Why do you believe the majority of women and men who experience discrimination and harassment keep silent about their experiences?

+ What kinds of advice would you offer a co-worker who confided in you that she was being sexually harassed by her supervisor?
+ What kinds of advice would you offer a co-worker who confided in you that he was being racially discriminated against by his supervisor?
+ Do you know your company's policy on nondiscrimination? On sexual harassment? Were you provided with training in these policies by your employer?
+ Have you ever witnessed harassing comments and gestures toward lesbians and/or gays? How did this make you feel?
+ Why do you believe sexual harassment is sometimes seen as a joke? What steps can you take to alert your friends and co-workers to the fact that sexual harassment is no laughing matter?

---

*In 1974, Mechelle Vinson sued her supervisor, Sidney Taylor, and her employer, Meritor Savings Bank, claiming that during her four years of employment at the bank she had been subjected to continuing sexually harassing behavior. Vinson stated that soon after she began working at Meritor, Taylor suggested they go to a motel for sex. She declined but after repeated requests on the part of Taylor and out of fear of losing her job, she agreed. Vinson claimed that Taylor made repeated demands upon her for sexual favors, usually at the bank branch during and after business hours. Vinson also stated that Taylor fondled her in front of other employees, followed her into the women's restroom when she went there alone, exposed himself to her, forcibly raped her on several occasions, and touched and fondled other women employees. Vinson's case went to the Supreme Court, which stated that certain conduct directed at women, whether or not it is directly linked to the grant or denial of an economic benefit, could constitute a violation of Title VII if the conduct "has the purpose or effect of unreasonably interfering with an individual's work performance or creating an intimidating, hostile, or offensive working environment."*

*Do you believe Mechelle Vinson experienced sexual harassment in her workplace? Why or why not?*

## SEXUAL HARASSMENT IN THE WORKPLACE

Sexual harassment is one type of sex discrimination that violates Title VII of the 1964 Civil Rights Act.[1] The Equal Employment Opportunity Commission (EEOC) has defined sexual harassment as "unwelcome sexual advances, requests for sexual favors, and other verbal or physical conduct of a sexual nature" when any one of the following criteria is met:

+ Submission to such conduct is made either explicitly or implicitly a term or condition of the individual's employment;
+ Submission to or rejection of such conduct by an individual is used as the basis for employment decisions affecting the individual;

+ Such conduct has the purpose or effect of unreasonably interfering with an individual's work performance or creating an intimidating, hostile, or offensive work environment.[2]

Two types of sexual harassment situations are described by this legal definition: *quid pro quo sexual harassment* and *hostile environment sexual harassment*.[3] *Quid pro quo sexual harassment* involves an individual with organizational power (e.g., a manager, a supervisor) who either expressly or implicitly ties an employment decision to the response of an individual to unwelcome sexual advances. Thus, a supervisor may promise a reward (e.g., a promotion) to an employee for complying with sexual requests or threaten an employee for failing to comply with sexual requests (e.g., threatening to not give the employee a promotion that has been earned). *Hostile environment sexual harassment* involves a situation where an atmosphere or climate is created in the office (or in another area in the workplace or at a company-sponsored event) that makes it difficult, if not impossible, for an employee to work because the atmosphere is perceived by the employee to be intimidating, offensive, and hostile, as in the case of Mechelle Vinson.

Thus, sexual harassment includes, but is not limited to, the following:[4]

+ Unwelcome sexual advances
+ Sexual innuendos, comments, and sexual remarks
+ Suggestive, obscene, or insulting sounds
+ Implied or expressed threat of reprisal for refusal to comply with a sexual request
+ Patting, pinching, brushing up against another's body
+ Sexually suggestive objects, books, magazines, posters, photographs, cartoons, e-mail, or pictures displayed in the work area
+ Actual denial of a work-related benefit for refusal to comply with sexual requests.

Sexual harassment can be physical, verbal, visual, or written. These behaviors constitute sexual harassment if they are committed by individuals who are in supervisory positions or who are peers.[5] These behaviors constitute sexual harassment if they occur between individuals of the same sex or between individuals of the opposite sex.[5]

## INCIDENCE OF WORKPLACE SEXUAL HARASSMENT

Social scientists have offered a behavioral definition of sexual harassment: unwanted sexually offensive behavior that threatens one's psychological health and well-being.[6] Several research studies have investigated this behavioral rather than legal aspect of sexual harassment by asking employees if they have experienced behaviors that illustrate unwanted sexual behaviors. For example, the U.S. Congress commissioned the largest study of sexual harassment to date. The U.S. Merit Systems Protection Board[7] surveyed a stratified random sample of 23,964 federal employees about their experiences with sexual harassment in the preceding two-year period. This study indicated that 42 percent of all women employees reported being sexually harassed. Merit Systems reported that many incidents occurred repeatedly, were of long duration, and had a sizable practical impact, costing the government an estimated minimum of $189 million over the two-year period covered by the research study. Thirty percent of the women reported receiving unwelcome sexual remarks, 26 percent stated they had been deliberately touched, and 28 percent reported suggestive looks. In addition, 15 percent had been pressured for dates, 9 percent had been pressured for sexual favors, and 9 percent had received unwelcome letters or phone calls. One percent of the women reported an actual or attempted rape. Merit Systems repeated their research six years later with essentially the same results.[8]

The Department of Defense (DoD)[9] conducted a survey in 1988 to assess sexual harassment among active duty military personnel. The DoD survey was modeled after the U.S. Merit Systems Protection Board survey. Of the 20,400 participants who completed the survey, 64 percent of the women and 17 percent of the men reported having experienced sexual harassment at least once during the previous 12 months.

In 1995, the DoD[10] surveyed the experiences of unwanted sexual behavior among active duty military personnel, based on adaptations of L. Fitzgerald and others' Sexual Experiences Questionnaire (SEQ).[11] Of the 28,296 participants who completed the SEQ-DoD survey, 76 percent of the women and 37 percent of the men reported having experienced some form of sexual harassment during the previous 12 months. Overall, these studies show that sexual harassment is much more common among women than among men.

B. Gutek's[12] research with women in the civilian workplace found that approximately half of the female workforce experiences sexual harassment. Based on telephone interviews generated by random digit dialing procedures, Gutek's results suggested that 53 percent of employed women have reported one incident of sexual harassment during their career, including degrading, insulting comments (15%), sexual touching (24%), socializing expected as part of the job requirement (11%), and expected sexual activity (8%).

Group differences in sexual harassment incidence rates have been noted. Fitzgerald and her colleagues,[13] for example, found that women who were employed in a university setting were more likely to experience sexual harassment than women students in the same institution. Y. Gold[14] found that blue-collar tradeswomen experienced significantly higher levels of all types of sexual harassment than did either white-collar professional women or pink-collar clerical women. Note that victims of sexual harassment also include men; however, only 15.1 percent of the sexual harassment charges were filed by men during 2004.[15] For certain employees the incidence of sexual harassment appears to be higher than others.[16] For example:

+ Women employees in male-populated careers
+ Women who are economically disadvantaged
+ Lesbian and gay employees
+ Employees with emotional or physical disabilities

Gutek[17] also noted that sexual harassment is more likely to occur in occupations in which "sex-role spillover" has occurred. When occupations are dominated by one sex or the other, the sex role of the dominant sex influences, that is, spills over into the work role expectations for that job. As an example, gender stereotypes imply that men should be sexually aggressive and women ready and willing to be sex objects. Sexual harassment can occur when these gender stereotypes carry over or spill over into the workplace setting. When employees act on their thoughts about women and men, they may engage in behavior that is discriminatory. Thus, the work environment becomes sexualized; it tolerates the expression of gender stereotyping, which fosters a hostile work environment because of the employee's sex.

Sexual harassment incidence rates have been consistently similar across different workplaces and parts of the United States, as well as across a nearly twenty-five-year span of research.[18] A. Barak[19] reviewed incidence data on workplace sexual harassment in several countries, including Australia, Canada, Egypt, Japan, Italy, Portugal, Sweden, Pakistan, Luxembourg, and Mexico. Barak noted that workplace sexual harassment is a "relatively widespread phenomenon across countries, continents, cultures, languages, and societies ... the form or the type of sexual harassment being carried out might be different in different countries."

## IMPACT OF SEXUAL HARASSMENT ON INDIVIDUALS AND THE WORKPLACE

The Equal Employment Opportunity Commission has interpreted the law to require that the effect and not the intent of sexually harassing behavior be the important consideration in determining whether a term or condition of employment is affected. The crux of a sexual harassment case is whether the employee found the behavior about which she or he is complaining to be unwelcome.[20] One way to determine the unwelcomeness of behavior is to look at the impact of such behavior on employees.[21] Research on sexual harassment has documented an impact on several areas of functioning, including emotional/psychological, physiological or health related, career/work, social, and self-perception.[22] Most victims experience severe distress associated with sexual harassment. The symptoms become exacerbated when the victim is in continued contact with the perpetrator, when the sexual harassment is carried out in front of co-workers, and when the victim is retaliated against for complaining about sexual harassment to the employer. Longitudinal research indicates that the negative effects of sexual harassment are enduring and often compounded by further sexual harassment.

Examples of emotional/psychological effects of sexual harassment include, but are not limited to, guilt, denial, withdrawal from social settings, shame, depression, fear, anger, anxiety, phobias, isolation, fear of crime, helplessness, frustration, shock, and decreased self-esteem.[23] The following are reported as physical/health-related effects of sexual harassment: headaches, tiredness, respiratory problems, substance abuse, sleep disturbances, eating disorders, lethargy, gastrointestinal disorders, dermatological reactions, and inability to concentrate.[24]

In addition, empirical research has indicated that victims of sexual harassment experience an impact on their career goals as well as on their ability to perform their job in the way to which they were accustomed. This impact includes, but is not limited to, changes in work habits, absenteeism, and changes in career goals.[25] The impact of sexual victimization on social and interpersonal relationships has included the following: withdrawal, fear of new people, lack of trust, changes in social network patterns, and relationship difficulties.[26] Finally, research has identified the following impact on self-perception from experiencing sexual harassment: poor self-concept, powerlessness, and isolation.[27]

These responses are identical to what employees who have experienced workplace violence report, for example, depression, sleep disturbance, and psychosomatic problems.[28] The impact of sexual harassment and workplace violence on the organization are also identical: physical withdrawal from work, increased absenteeism, decreased morale, and a search for alternative employment opportunities.[29] Sexual harassment and workplace violence can also cost organizations millions of dollars due to employees' impaired concentration, reduced organizational commitment and productivity, and increased intragroup conflict, as well as reduced team cohesion and team performance and reduced job satisfaction.

## REPORTING SEXUAL HARASSMENT

Individuals may respond to sexual harassment in two major ways: internally and externally.[30] Internal strategies represent attempts to manage the personal emotions and cognitions associated with the behaviors they experienced. Internally focused strategies identified by researchers include the following:

*Detachment:* Employee minimizes the situation and treats it as a joke.

*Denial:* Employee denies behaviors; attempts to forget about them.

*Relabeling:* Employee reappraises the situation as less threatening, and offers excuses for the harasser's behavior.

*Illusory Control:* Employee attempts to take responsibility for the harassment.

*Endurance:* Employee puts up with behavior, either because she/he does not believe help is available or because she fears retaliation.

Externally focused strategies focus on the harassing situation itself, including reporting the behavior to the individual charged with investigating complaints of sexual harassment. Externally focused strategies include the following:

*Avoidance:* Employee attempts to avoid the situation by staying away from the harasser.

*Assertion/Confrontation:* Employee refuses sexual or social offers or verbally confronts the harasser.

*Seeking Institutional/Organizational Relief:* Employee reports the incident and files a complaint.

*Social Support:* Employee seeks the support of others to validate perceptions of the behavior.

*Appeasement:* Employee attempts to evade the harasser without confrontation, and attempts to placate the harasser.

Most individuals who have experienced sexual harassment at work use the internally focused strategies.[31] They typically do not tell the perceived harasser to stop. Their initial attempts to manage the perceived harasser are rarely direct. Typically, harassers are more powerful organizationally and physically than the victims, and sometimes the harasser's intentions are unclear. The first or first few harassing events are often ignored by victims, especially when they are experiencing hostile environment sexual harassment where the behavior may be subtle.[31] Victims may interpret or reinterpret the situation so that the incident is not defined as sexual harassment. Furthermore, victims of sexual harassment fear retaliation should they confront the harasser. The economic reality for most employees is that they cannot just leave a workplace where they are being sexually harassed.[31]

## CONSENSUAL RELATIONSHIPS

Consensual relationships,[32] while not illegal, potentially cause difficulties for organizations for the following reasons:

+ The situation involves one person exerting power over another.
+ The seduction of a much younger individual is usually involved.
+ Conflict of interest issues arise, e.g., how can a supervisor fairly evaluate an employee with whom she/he is having a sexual relationship?

+ The potential for exploitation and abuse is high.
+ The potential for retaliatory harassment is high when the sexual relationship ceases.
+ Other individuals may be affected and make accusations of favoritism.[33]

Employers may issue a policy banning consensual relationships, especially when the manager or supervisor has some organizational power over the employee. All managers have an ethical and professional responsibility to provide an environment that is respectful of employees and fosters their work performance. The stories employees tell about their consensual relationships do not parallel romances or sexual affairs. Rather, they resemble stories depicting patterns of manipulation and victimization, responses identical to those from women who are sexually harassed in a nonconsensual relationship.[34] Sample consensual relationship policies are presented at the end of this chapter.

## WHY SEXUAL HARASSMENT OCCURS

Research has indicated that men are more likely to sexually harass than women.[35] The incidence of female-female sexual harassment and female-male sexual harassment is small, compared to male-female sexual harassment. When men are sexually harassed, it is usually another male who engages in the behavior. Research has challenged the belief that there is a "typical harasser."[36] Men who sexually harass are found in all occupations and are of all age groups. Sexual harassment, like rape, incest, and intimate partner abuse, is characterized by aggression, power, dominance, and force.[36] Men who sexually harass are not pathological but exhibit behaviors characteristic of the masculine gender role in the United States.[36]

The element of aggression that is so deeply embedded in the masculine gender role is present in sexual harassment.[37] For many men, aggression is one of the major ways to "prove" their masculinity, especially among those men who feel some sense of powerlessness in their lives. The theme of male-as-dominant or male-as-aggressor is so central to many men's self-concepts that it literally carries over into their interpersonal communications, especially with women co-workers. Sexualizing a professional relationship may be the one way that such a man can still prove his masculinity when he can find few other ways to prove himself in control or to be the dominant person in a relationship.

Michele Paludi[38] noted that while the focus has been on men's attitudes toward women, it would be more helpful to study men's attitudes toward other men, competition, and power. Men often act out of extreme competitiveness, ego, or fear of losing their positions of power. They do not want to appear weak or less masculine in the eyes of other men so they engage in the "scoping of women," making implied or overt threats, or spying on women. Women are the objects of the game designed to impress other men. When men are encouraged to be obsessionally competitive and concerned with dominance, it is likely that they will eventually use violent means to achieve dominance.

In theorizing about why sexual harassment occurs, researchers have all acknowledged the power differential between sexual harassers and victims of sexual harassment.[39] The reality is that sexual harassment occurs anywhere once communal barriers—the sense of mutual regard and the obligations of civility—are lowered by actions that seem to signal that "no one cares." We note that the "broken windows"[40] theory can be applied to workplaces trying to prevent and deal with workplace violence. If what is perceived by the organization to be trivial is not handled immediately, more severe forms of workplace violence may result (see below).

---

### Meet Dr. William Schweinle

My research has focused on wife-directed aggression and sexual harassment. Both of these men's behaviors are associated with a bias on the men's part to perceive women as being critical or rejecting when the women are not actually having those sentiments. These findings suggest that men's aggression against women may be generally linked to more aggressive men's biased social perception, and that sexual harassment may be a form of aggression—not seduction. So, to reduce workplace aggression in the form of sexual harassment, I would suggest that everyone take note of men who seem hypersensitive to rejection or criticism and who seem to infer criticism or rejection erroneously. Not hiring these men might be the best prevention.

Dr. William E. Schweinle is director of academic evaluation and assessment and assistant professor of psychology at the University of South Dakota.

---

## EMPLOYER SUPPORT

In addition to the internally and externally focused strategies discussed earlier, there are characteristics of organizations that are most likely to have a high incidence of sexual harassment. Such organizations are likely not to do the following:[41]

+ Disseminate and/or enforce the policy statement prohibiting sexual harassment or report information regarding sexual harassment
+ Have adequate training for employees
+ Intervene officially when sexual harassment occurs
+ Support sexual harassment victims
+ Give sanctions to individuals who engage in sexual harassment
+ Inform the organization about the sanctions for offenders

The EEOC has emphasized that an employer has an affirmative duty to issue a strong policy statement prohibiting sexual harassment, a policy statement on which employees are trained; conduct a full investigation of all complaints of sexual harassment; and take appropriate disciplinary action against individuals who have violated the policy statement.[42] Research has suggested that without training in harassment awareness, individuals who engage in this form of victimization are likely to be repeat offenders.[43] A sample policy with investigatory procedures is presented at the end of this chapter. The components of effective policy statements that have been identified with respect to sexual harassment are the following:[44]

+ Statement of purpose
+ Legal definition
+ Behavioral examples
+ Statement concerning impact of discrimination on individuals and workplace
+ Statement of individual's responsibility in filing complaint
+ Statement of workplace's responsibility in investigating complaint
+ Statement concerning confidentiality of complaint procedures
+ Statement concerning sanctions available
+ Statement of sanctions for retaliation
+ Statement concerning false complaints
+ Identification and background of individual(s) responsible for hearing complaints

Several components for effective complaint procedures have been identified in the  sexual harassment literature. These include all of the following at a minimum:[45]

a. Informing employees that the workplace will not ignore any complaint of discrimination and harassment
b. Informing employees that the investigator of complaints will not make determinations about the complaint based on the reputations or organizational status of the individuals involved
c. Informing employees that investigations of complaints will be completed promptly
d. Informing employees that witnesses to incidents and/or to changes in the parties' behavior will be interviewed
e. Informing employees that all documents presented by the complainant, alleged harasser, and witnesses will be reviewed
f. Informing employees that the complainant and the accused will be interviewed in detail

The Equal Employment Opportunity Commission[42] has stated that a vital part of the harassment policy statement informs employees what sanctions will be imposed if they violate the policy statement. Discipline should be designed to end the sexual harassment and prevent it from reoccurring.

Specific examples of progressive discipline should be provided in the policy statement and procedures, including verbal warning, written reprimand in the harasser's personnel file, pay increase denials, pay reduction, transfer of the harasser, demotion, or dismissal. Employees should also be reminded that the sexual harassment policy provides for stricter penalties for continued misbehavior.[44]

It is recommended that the policy statement be reissued each year by the company president as well as displayed prominently throughout the organization.[44] In addition, the policy statement should be published in employee handbooks. The responsibility for communicating the policy statement must be made a part of the job description of anyone with authority in the organization. It is also recommended that employees sign a statement that they have been given a copy of the policy, that they understand it, and that they have been trained on it. The names and contact information for sexual harassment investigators should also be publicized and made easy to find on the organization's Web site. In addition, managers must be taught to intervene when they observe sexual harassment.

The absence of an effective sexual harassment policy using training programs means that employees will not fully comprehend what behaviors do, in fact, constitute harassment and retaliation, and will not understand clearly how their employer will deal with complaints and sanctions for violating the policy.

Michele Paludi and Carmen Paludi have also provided the following recommendations with respect to effective sexual harassment policy statements:[44]

+ The policy should be drafted in sex-neutral terms.
+ The policy statement must contain an alternative procedure for complaints if the investigator or supervisor is the alleged harasser.
+ A woman and a man should be named as co-investigators of sexual harassment complaints.
+ Claims of sexual harassment should not be trivialized but treated seriously. All claims must be thoroughly investigated before any action is taken. Should an individual felt that she/he is in physical danger, changes must be made in the workplace. Suggestions for notifying police must also be provided.
+ The policy statement must be available in other languages in addition to English.
+ The policy statement must be revised when new case law and state law modifications make revisions necessary.
+ Employees should be involved in the development of a sexual harassment policy statement.
+ The policy must state how, when, and by whom the policy will be monitored, evaluated, and reviewed.
+ All those involved in the workplace must be committed to the policy.
+ The policy must be applied consistently.

## TRAINING PROGRAMS

Workplaces are required to take reasonable steps to prevent and end sexual harassment of employees, including the facilitation of training programs on sexual harassment awareness.[45] Training programs involve more than a recitation of individuals' rights and responsibilities and the requirements of the law and of workplace policy. Training also requires dealing with individuals' assumptions and misconceptions about power as well as their anxieties about the training itself.[44] Stereotypes about men, women, sex, and power often remain unchallenged unless individuals participate in effective trainer-guided intervention programs.

In addition, training programs on sexual harassment must provide all individuals with a clear understanding of their rights and responsibilities with respect to sexual harassment.[44] Training must also enable individuals to distinguish between behavior that is sexual harassment and behavior that is not sexual harassment. Training programs also provide individuals with information concerning the policy statement against sexual harassment and the investigatory procedures set up by the workplace. Finally, training programs have as their goal to help empower individuals to use their organization's procedures for resolving complaints.[46]

If employers tolerate sexual harassment of their employees, they are also more likely to tolerate workplace violence, and vice versa.[39] Attention must be given by the employer to all forms of organizational abuse, including sexual harassment and workplace violence.

Having an effective and enforced policy, procedures, and training program will show that the organization cares about its employees and provide a strong foundation for prevention that will ensure that employees have the right to receive equal employment opportunities. We return to this issue in chapter 7.

### Policy Statement on Sexual Harassment

(Name of Company) has an obligation to create a work environment for all employees that is fair, humane, and responsible—an environment that supports, nurtures, and rewards career progress on the basis of such relevant factors as work performance.

All employees of (Name of Company) have the responsibility to cooperate in creating a climate at (Name of Company) where sexual harassment does not occur. We have zero tolerance for sexual harassment of our employees. No employees at any levels of (Name of Company) may engage in sexual harassment.

The following policy statement is designed to help employees of (Name of Company) become aware of behavior that is sexual harassment and the procedures (Name of Company) will use to deal with sexual harassment in such a way as to protect complainants, witnesses, and respondents.

*What is Sexual Harassment?*

Sexual harassment is legally defined as "unwelcome sexual advances, requests for sexual favors, and other verbal or physical conduct of a sexual nature" when any one of the following criteria is met:

+ Submission to such conduct is made either explicitly or implicitly a term or condition of the individual's employment;
+ Submission to or rejection of such conduct by an individual is used as the basis for employment decisions affecting the individual;
+ Such conduct has the purpose or effect of unreasonably interfering with an individual's work performance or creating an intimidating, hostile, or offensive work environment.

Two types of sexual harassment situations are described by this legal definition: *quid pro quo sexual harassment* and *hostile environment sexual harassment.*

*Quid pro quo sexual harassment* involves an individual with organizational power who either expressly or implicitly ties an employment decision to the response of an employee to unwelcome sexual advances. Thus, a supervisor may promise a reward to an employee for complying with sexual requests (e.g., a better job, promotion, a raise) or threaten an employee's job for failing to comply with sexual requests (e.g., threatening not to promote the employee, threatening to give an unsatisfactory performance appraisal).

*Hostile environment sexual harassment* involves a situation where an atmosphere or climate is created in the workplace that makes it difficult, if not impossible, for an employee to work because the atmosphere is perceived by the employee to be intimidating, offensive, and hostile.

For the purposes of this policy, sexual harassment includes, but is not limited to, the following:

+ Unwelcome sexual advances
+ Sexual innuendos, comments, and sexual remarks
+ Suggestive, obscene, or insulting sounds
+ Implied or expressed threat of reprisal for refusal to comply with a sexual request
+ Patting, pinching, brushing up against another's body
+ Sexually suggestive objects, books, magazines, poster, photographs, cartoons, e-mail, or pictures displayed in the work area
+ Actual denial of a job-related benefit for refusal to comply with sexual requests

Thus, sexual harassment can be physical, verbal, visual, or written. These behaviors constitute sexual harassment if they are committed by individuals who are in supervisory positions or who are co-workers. And these behaviors constitute sexual harassment if they occur between individuals of the same sex or between individuals of the opposite sex. (Name of Company) prohibits these and other forms of sexual harassment. Any employee who engages in such behavior will be subject to disciplinary procedures.

*What Is Not Sexual Harassment?*

Sexual harassment does not refer to relationships between responsible, consenting adults. Sexual harassment does not mean flirting. Giving compliments does not mean sexual harassment. Sexual harassment refers to unwanted, unwelcome behavior. Not every joke or touch or comment is sexual harassment. The key is to determine if the behavior is unwanted and unwelcome. Furthermore, sexual harassment interferes with an employee's ability to get his or her work done.

*Costs of Sexual Harassment*

There are high costs of sexual harassment for individuals. They include depression, feelings of helplessness, headaches, anxiety, sleep disturbances, and disordered eating. The cost of sexual harassment to our company includes decreased productivity, absenteeism, and decreased morale.

*What Should Individuals Do If They Believe They Are Being Sexually Harassed?*

Employees who have complaints of sexual harassment, including sexual harassment by any supervisor, co-worker, vendor, client, or visitor, are urged to report such conduct to (Name of Investigator) so that (s)he may investigate and resolve the problem. Employees are encouraged to bring their concerns to (Name of Investigator) within 60 days of the alleged incident(s). Employees may ask (Name of Investigator) to postpone an investigation if the performance appraisal of the employee will be performed by the party against whom the complaint is brought.

(Name of Investigator) will investigate all complaints as expeditiously as possible in a professional manner. The confidentiality of the investigative procedures will be maintained. The complaint will be investigated and resolved typically within a two-week period.

Complainants and those against whom complaints have been filed will not be expected to meet together to discuss the resolution of the complaint.

Investigatory procedures have been developed and are fully explained in another memorandum: (Name of Company) Sexual Harassment Complaint Procedure.

Any employee who is found to have engaged in sexual harassment will be subject to disciplinary action, as indicated in (Name of Company's) complaint procedure.

*Discussions about Sexual Harassment: These Are Not Complaints*

Employees at (Name of Company) have the right to seek advice and information about sexual harassment from (Name of Investigator), who will maintain such consultation in confidence. Such discussions do not constitute filing a complaint of sexual harassment.

*Retaliation*

There will be no retaliation against employees for reporting sexual harassment or assisting (Name of Investigator) in the investigation of a complaint. Any retaliation against such individuals is subject to disciplinary action, including verbal and written reprimands, transfers, demotions, and dismissal.

### False Complaints

If after investigating any complaint of sexual harassment it is discovered that the complaint is not bona fide or that an individual has provided false information regarding the complaint, that individual may be subject to disciplinary action, including verbal and written reprimands, transfers, demotions, and dismissal.

### Recommended Corrective Action

The purpose of any recommended corrective action to resolve a complaint will be to correct or remedy the injury, if any, to the complainant and to prevent further harassment. Recommended action may include the following: a private or public apology, written or oral reprimand of the individual who engaged in sexual harassment, relief from specific duties, suspension, transfer, or dismissal of the individual who engaged in sexual harassment.

If complainants are not satisfied with the attempts to resolve the sexual harassment, they may seek resolution through other sources, for example, the (Name of State) Division of Human Rights or the Equal Employment Opportunity Commission.

### Policy Review

This policy will be reviewed periodically by (Name of Investigator) and by (Name of President), who welcome comments on the policy, its interpretation, or its implementation.

For additional information regarding sexual harassment, contact (Name of Investigator) or (Name of President). They have been trained in complaint resolution and receive additional education about sexual harassment law and its management and psychological applications. Both (Name of Investigator) and (Name of President) will be responsible for a program of information and education concerning this policy and procedures relating to sexual harassment.

Office Numbers and Phone Numbers:

(Of Investigator)

(Of President)

### Sexual Harassment Complaint Procedure

Employees of (Name of Company) who have complaints of sexual harassment by anyone at this company, including any supervisors, are encouraged to report such conduct to (Name of Investigator) so that (s)he may investigate and resolve the problem. Individuals who believe they have been subjected to sexual harassment should report the circumstances orally and/or in writing within 60 days to (Name of Investigator).

(Name of Investigator) will maintain confidentiality in her/his investigation of complaints of sexual harassment.

Any employee pursuing a complaint may do so without fear of reprisal.

*Informal Advice and Consultation*

Employees may seek informal assistance or advice from (Name of Investigator). All such consultations will be confidential and no action involving any individual beyond (Name of Investigator) and the employee will be taken until a formal complaint has been made.

(Name of Investigator) may, however, take action, within the context of the company's existing policy and procedures, that (s)he deems appropriate on the basis of information received, to protect all employees of (Name of Company).

*Resolution of Informal Complaints*

Any employee may discuss an informal complaint with (Name of Investigator). If the employee who discusses an informal complaint is not willing to be identified to the person against whom the informal complaint is made, (Name of Investigator) will make a confidential record of the circumstances and will provide guidance about various ways to resolve the problem.

If the employee bringing the complaint is willing to be identified to the person against whom the complaint is made and wishes to attempt an informal resolution of the problem, (Name of Investigator) will make a confidential record of the circumstances (signed by the complainant) and undertake appropriate discussions with the person complained about.

When a number of people report incidents of sexual harassment that have occurred in a public context (for example, offensive sexual remarks in an office setting) or when (Name of Investigator) has received repeated complaints from various employees that an individual has engaged in sexual harassment, the person complained against will be informed without the identity of the complainants being revealed.

*Resolution of Formal Complaints*

If an employee wishes to pursue the matter through formal resolution, a written complaint must be submitted to (Name of Investigator), giving details of the alleged harassment, including dates, times, places, name(s) of individual(s) involved, and names of any witnesses.

The complaint must be addressed to (Name of Investigator).

Formal complaints will be investigated in the following manner:

Upon receipt of a written complaint, (Name of Investigator) will immediately forward a copy of the complaint, along with a copy of (Name of Company's) Sexual Harassment Policy Statement and Procedures, to the individual complained against and request a meeting within three days.

The investigation will be limited to what is necessary to resolve the complaint or make a recommendation. If it appears necessary for (Name of Investigator) to speak to any individuals other than those involved in the complaint, (s)he will do so only after informing the complainant and the person complained against.

(Name of Investigator) will investigate all complaints of sexual harassment expeditiously and professionally. To the extent that this is possible, the investigation will be completed within two weeks from the time the formal investigation is initiated.

(Name of Investigator) will also maintain the confidentiality of the information provided to her/him in the complaint and investigation process. The only other employee of (Name of Company) who will be informed about the investigation is (Name of President), President of (Name of Company).

(Name of Company's) first priority will be to attempt to resolve the complaint through the mutual agreement of the complainant and the person complained against.

If an employee making a formal complaint asks not to be identified until a later date (e.g., until the completion of a performance appraisal), (Name of Investigator) will decide whether or not to hold the complaint without further action until the date requested.

If a formal complaint has been preceded by an informal investigation, (Name of Investigator) shall decide whether there are sufficient grounds to warrant a formal investigation.

The names or other identifying information regarding witnesses for either party involved in the complaint will not be made known to the opposing party.

Referrals to therapists and medical personnel for all individuals involved in an investigation will be made available upon request.

Following the completion of an investigation, (Name of Investigator) will make one of the following determinations:

Sustain the Complaint: A finding of sexual harassment has been made and recommendations for corrective action will be identified. Recommended corrective action may include an apology, written or oral reprimand, relief from specific duties, suspension, dismissal, or transfer of the employee found to have engaged in sexual harassment.

Not Sustain the Complaint: A finding of no sexual harassment has been made.

Insufficient Information: Insufficient information exists on which to make a determination. (Name of Investigator) will reinvestigate all parties named in the complaint.

Following any determination and recommendations for corrective action, (Name of Investigator) will issue a written decision with findings of fact and reason to (Name of President). (Name of President) will correspond with the complainant and the person complained against, informing them of the findings of the investigation and recommendations for corrective action. Appropriate statements of apology will be made to employees involved in the complaint by (Name of President).

If complainants are not satisfied with the attempts to resolve their complaint of sexual harassment, they may seek resolution through other sources, for example, the (Name of State) Division of Human Rights or the Equal Employment Opportunity Commission.

For additional information regarding (Name of Company's) zero tolerance of sexual harassment, contact

Name of Investigator
Office Number
Phone Number
Name of President

Office Number

Phone Number

Both (Name of Investigator) and (Name of President) are trained in complaint resolution and receive additional education about sexual harassment law and its management and psychological applications.

In addition, (Name of President) and (Name of Investigator) will be responsible for a program of information and education concerning sexual harassment in general and (Name of Company's) policy and procedures.

### Examples of Consensual Relationship Policies

*Discouragement Policy*

At _____, amorous relationships between employees or between employees and clients or vendors, are deemed very unwise. We recommend against such relationships when one employee has direct authority over the other employee. If any work-related problems develop from such a relationship, the employee who holds the greater organizational power will be held entirely responsible.

*Prohibition Policy*

At _____, no supervisor will have an amorous relationship with another employee who is in any reporting relationship to said supervisor or whose work is being directly evaluated by said supervisor.

*Total Ban Policy*

At _____, no amorous relationship between supervisors and employees will be tolerated. This policy extends to supervisors who are not evaluating an employee currently or who are not in any reporting relationship with said employee currently.

*Potential Conflict of Interest Policy*

At _____, we recognize that supervisor-employee relationships are asymmetric in nature. Therefore, amorous relationships between supervisors and employees can lead to difficulties. In such relationships, the supervisor faces serious conflicts of interest, and must distance him/herself from any employment decisions involving the employee. Failure to do so will constitute a violation of an ethical obligation to the employee and to _____.

## RESOURCES

Contrada, R., Ashmore, R., Gary, M., Coups, E., Egeth, J., Sewell, A., Ewell, K., & Goyal, T. (2000). Ethnicity-related sources of stress and their effects on well being. *Current Directions in Psychological Science*, 9, 136–139.

Dansky, B., & Kilpatrick, D. (1997). Effects of sexual harassment. In W. O'Donohue (Ed.), *Sexual harassment: Theory, research, and practice* (pp.151–174). Boston: Allyn & Bacon.

Fiske, S., & Stevens, L. (1993). What's so special about sex? Gender stereotyping and discrimination. In S. Oskamp & M. Costanzo (Eds.), *Gender issues in contemporary society* (pp. 173–196). Newbury Park, CA: Sage.

Levy, A., & Paludi, M. (2002). *Workplace sexual harassment.* Upper Saddle River, NJ: Prentice Hall.

U.S. Department of Justice, Federal Bureau of Investigation. *Hate Crimes Report* Retrieved from http://www.fbi.gov/ucr/hatecm.htm.

## Associations Dealing with Harassment

www.hatecrimes.org
www.civilrights.org

Equal Employment Opportunity Commission
http://www.eeoc.gov
1801 L Street, NW
Washington, DC 20507

Feminist Majority Foundation
http://www.feminist.org
1600 Wilson Boulevard, Suite 801
Arlington, VA 222095

National Council on Crime and Delinquency
*Hate Crime Prevention Resource Guide*
685 Market St., Suite 620
San Francisco, CA 94105
415–896–6223

U.S. Department of Justice
Community Relations Service
600 E St., NW
Washington, DC 20530

# CHAPTER 6

# Intimate Partner Violence as a Workplace Concern

Domestic violence causes far more pain than the visible marks of bruises and scars. It is devastating to be abused by someone that you love and think loves you in return. It is estimated that approximately 3 million incidents of domestic violence are reported each year in the United States.
—Dianne Feinstein

Sexual, racial, gender violence and other forms of discrimination and violence in a culture cannot be eliminated without changing culture.
—Charlotte Bunch

Millions of women, children, and families are better off as a result of having the Violence Against Women Act in place.
—Chris Chocola

Through education, improved funding and support, we can continue to work together to provide safe environments for victims and end the cycle of domestic violence.
—Jerry Moran

### Questions for Reflection

+ How do you define domestic violence?
+ Do you believe workplaces should get involved in domestic disputes between an employee and his/her mate/spouse? Why or why not?

+ If you needed your employer to assist you because you were being stalked by an ex-spouse, what would you request of your employer?
+ Do you believe domestic violence has an impact on children who witness the battering? Why or why not?
+ Do you have available the phone numbers of the following organizations/individuals in your community?
Clergy
Police
Domestic violence shelter
Employee assistance program associated with your workplace

---

*Barbara Cavalier had been married to her husband, Chris Cavalier, for seven years. During the course of their marriage, Chris had been abusive toward Barbara. When he put a gun to her head, she decided to leave him. For six months her living arrangements were kept secret. One day Chris walked into the Elmwood siding supply business and saw Barbara where she was working as a data entry clerk. Subsequently, Chris walked into the store, armed with two guns, a .45 caliber automatic pistol and a .357 caliber Magnum revolver. Chris killed Barbara and her co-worker, Stephanie Revolta, who had tried to defuse the situation. Stephanie had placed a 911 call but by the time assistance arrived, Barbara and Stephanie were dead. Chris also took his own life. Barbara's co-workers reported that Chris had been harassing Barbara all day, calling her at work and stealing her truck. Authorities had found a note in Chris's house in which he assigned power of attorney and listed valuables that he wanted to give away. This behavior led police to believe that Chris had planned the murders that day.*

Homicide is *the* leading cause of occupational death for women. Approximately 2,600,000 women are victims of workplace violence annually.[1] Women who are victims of violence perpetrated by their mates account for one-quarter of all women who are murdered in a given year. Furthermore, more women in the United States are victimized by their male partner than are harmed because of reported muggings, automobile accidents, and rapes combined.[2] Thus, while employment may provide an escape from the victimization women experience outside the workplace by their mates, it also offers a site where the batterer, like Barbara Cavalier's husband, can consistently find his victim. Thus, domestic violence spills over into the workplace.

## DOMESTIC VIOLENCE

Domestic violence has been noted throughout history. In the Old Testament, a husband could have his wife put to death for her unfaithfulness and his children beaten or killed for breaking the injunction to "honor thy father and mother." The phrase "rule of thumb" has its roots in intimate partner violence. The phrase originated from English common law; it reflected a law that allowed a husband to beat his wife with a stick or whip no larger than the diameter of his thumb.

Domestic violence, also referred to as battering, spouse abuse, spousal assault, and intimate partner abuse, is defined as violence between adults who are intimates, regardless of their marital status, living arrangements, or sexual orientations.[2] Such violence includes throwing, shoving, and slapping as well as beatings, forced sex, threats with a deadly weapon, and homicide.[3] Abuse in couples' relationships may also include intense criticisms and put-downs, verbal harassment, intimidation, restraint of normal activities and freedoms, and denial of access to resources.[4] Thus, violence can be physical, emotional and, sexual and is used by one partner to control another.[5]

Violence in couples appears during adolescence and young adulthood as well as middle and later adulthood.[6] Research suggests that battering in dating relationships affects one-third of U.S. college and university students.[7] In dating relationships, women experience being pushed, grabbed, or shoved by their male dates. In addition, both female and male students report being slapped and having objects thrown at them, and being stalked by ex-lovers who refuse to accept the end of the relationship.[6]

Research involving more than 8,000 families has suggested that one out of every six couples engage in at least one violent act each year.[8] Over the course of a relationship, just over one-fourth of couples will experience intimate partner violence. This research concluded that "The American family and the American home are perhaps as or more violent than any other American institution or setting (with the exception of the military, and only then in time of war)."[8]

## INTERNATIONAL RESEARCH

In 1995, the Fourth United Nations International Conference on Women concluded: "In all societies ... women and girls are subjected to physical, sexual and psychological abuse that cuts across lines of income, class and culture."[9] This conference did not identify any country that did not have domestic violence. Carolee Tran and Kunya Des Jardins[10] reported that the incidence of domestic violence experienced in Vietnamese refugee and Korean immigrant communities is similar to that in the United States as a whole. Junko Kozu[11] reported that domestic violence is prevalent in Japan. Kozu included elder abuse and filial violence in her definition of domestic violence. Sharon Horne[12] concluded from her research on domestic violence in Russia that it exceeds Western rates by four or five times. In the first research study on domestic violence among women and men in Greece, Christina Antonopoulou[13] reported that the majority of participants in her study had experienced domestic violence throughout childhood and adolescence. In addition, domestic violence is prevalent in all races and ethnic groups and among women in urban, rural, and suburban areas.

## SEX AND SEXUAL ORIENTATION VARIABLES

While women are more likely to be victims of battering, men may be battered by women.[14] The reasons for battering are different by sex. Men tend to batter because they want control in the relationship; women tend to batter in self-defense because of fear of being killed. More women are seriously injured and killed by male batterers than men are by female batterers.[14] There has been a relative paucity of research on lesbian and gay relationships and violence. Research has suggested that the incidence of same-sex battering may be similar to that of heterosexual battering.[15]

## SILENCE SURROUNDING DOMESTIC VIOLENCE

The incidence rates reported thus far are an underrepresentation, since intimate partner violence is a relatively hidden form of violence. Attesting to the privatization of family violence, the first book to examine this form of victimization was entitled *Scream Quietly or the Neighbors Will Hear*.[16] Intimate partner violence is a taboo topic, and many individuals do not admit to its existence. Thus, many victims fail to report the violence. In addition, police officers and judges may dismiss intimate partner violence as inconsequential. Homophobic attitudes prevent lesbian and gay victims of battering from reporting their experiences to the police. They would have to disclose their sexual orientation to the police if they disclosed the violence. Disclosure may be resisted due to their concerns about retaliation against themselves, their family members, and their children.[15]

## CYCLE OF BATTERING

From their use of violence, men who batter gain personal feelings of power and control. They control a woman's whereabouts and demand to know everything about her experiences at home and at work or school. A cyclical pattern of beating is common. Lenore Walker[17] identified three phases within this cycle. In the tension-building phase, there are battering incidents. The woman attempts to avoid escalation of the battering by trying to "calm" her mate and by staying out of his way. The tension becomes too high to be controlled by these efforts, and the batterer responds with an acute battering incident in the second phase. In phase three, the tension from the first two phases is gone and the batterer becomes "charming" toward the woman. He delivers apologies and promises never to batter again. The duration of these phases vary from couple to couple. The level of violence tends to increase both in frequency and severity as the relationship continues over time.

Research has identified several individual vulnerability factors related to domestic violence,[18] including: history of physical abuse, prior injury from the same partner, economic stress, having a verbally abusive partner, partner history of alcohol and/or drug use, and childhood abuse. Relational vulnerability factors related to domestic violence include marital conflict, marital instability, male dominance in the family, and dysfunction of the family.

Several myths exist surrounding domestic violence. For example:

+ Children are not affected by watching their parents in a battering relationship.
+ There are no long-term consequences of battering.
+ People must enjoy the battering since they rarely leave the abusive relationship.

We will discuss each of these myths, countering them with the realities of domestic violence.

### Myth: Children Are Not Affected by Watching Their Parents in a Battering Relationship.

*Reality:* Children are often in the middle of domestic violence.[19] Each year, at least 3.3 million children in the United States, between the ages of 3 and 17 years, are at risk of exposure to their mothers being battered by their fathers.[19] In addition, children may be neglected by their mothers, who may be too emotionally and physically abused even to help themselves.[18] Furthermore, children may be injured indirectly when household objects are thrown or weapons are used in the violence. Intimate partner violence may be the single major precursor to child abuse and neglect fatalities in this country.[19]

Commonly, older children are injured when attempting to intervene in the victimization to protect their mothers. Children may also be abused by the violent parent.[20] Homicide is one of the five leading causes of child mortality in the United States. In addition, threats against children are often used by the batterer to control the behavior of their mother.

Child witnesses to domestic violence experience depression, anxiety, fear, and guilt for causing the abuse and not being able to prevent it.[20]

In addition, children feel guilty because they still love the abuser, who still provides food and shelter for them. Furthermore, children who witness domestic violence are at greater risk for drug abuse, juvenile delinquency, and suicide. Domestic violence contributes to adolescents' decisions to run away from home. Recently, Sandra Graham-Bermann and Julie Seng studied low-income preschool children in Michigan.[21] They found that 46.7 percent of the children in the study had been exposed to at least one incident of intimate partner violence in their family. These children suffered symptoms of post-traumatic stress disorder, including bed-wetting and nightmares, and they were at greater risk for asthma, gastrointestinal problems, and headaches than children not exposed to this victimization. Children exposed to domestic violence are in need of direct intervention since they have behavioral and emotional problems as a consequence of the violence.[19] Children's learning and nurturing are also affected by domestic violence.[19]

Children may also grow up to repeat the behavior patterns they witnessed in their parents.[22] Domestic violence is a learned behavior and is passed from one generation to the next. Children learn to resolve conflict through aggression and violence.

Fetuses are at risk from intimate partner violence as well.[23] Studies have indicated that approximately 324,000 pregnant women in the United States are battered by their mate or spouse. Complications of pregnancy are significantly higher for women who are battered than for women who are not. These complications include low weight gain, suicide attempts, alcohol and drug use, anemia, depression, infections, and first and second trimester bleeding.

**Myth: There Are No Long-Term Consequences of Battering.**

*Reality:* There are significant long-term consequences of battering, including depression, anger, fear, anxiety, irritability, post-traumatic stress disorder, loss of self-esteem, feelings of humiliation and alienation, and a sense of vulnerability.[18] Furthermore, the injuries that the battered individual receives include bruises, cuts, concussions, black eyes, broken bones, burns that leave scars, knife wounds, loss of hearing and/or vision, and joint damage.[18] The effects of violence on women's employment are significant as well, including absenteeism, termination, and difficulty in sustaining jobs throughout the remainder of their employment career.[1]

L. Friedman and S. Crouper[24] first studied the impact of domestic violence on women's employment. Of the 50 women they interviewed, 54 percent reported missing three days of work per month because of the violence, and 56 percent reported having lost a job because of it. Similar results were obtained by Stephanie Riger and her colleagues,[25] who found that of the 57 women residing in a domestic violence shelter in Chicago who were employed, 85 percent missed work because of the abuse and 53 percent were dismissed or had to leave because of the victimization.

Recently, Jennifer Swanberg and T. K. Logan[1] found that on-the-job interference tactics used by violent husbands or mates were the most detrimental to women's ability to do their jobs. Swanberg and Logan offered women's accounts of how their experiences at home spilled over into the workplace. For example:

Between the fighting all night and it's kind of hard to function properly. I'd go to work, but my job performance was not up to par and I was a cashier so that's pretty ... they did [notice] ... they come right out and say it.... I eventually had to leave.

He would call and I wasn't allowed to have personal phone calls so he'd get angry with that ... he'd eventually come out to work, the last time he showed up at work he dragged me out of work. My employer got tired of it and fired me.

He'd walk into [my] office and you know it's just a little tiny room. It sat between the two bathrooms. It was like a broom closet.... He would show up at my work and just the sight of him would tear me all to pieces. My manager did ask me one time, what's going on you know with you and man friend? I said, you know, we're having difficulties. She said we just don't want to have him coming in here interfering with your job. I eventually quit, because he would not stop coming to my job, I felt too ashamed.

**Myth: People Must Enjoy the Battering Since They Rarely Leave the Abusive Relationship.**

*Reality:* Very often victims of battering do leave the relationship.[18] Women and men remain in a battering relationship not because they are masochistic, but for several well-founded reasons, for example, threats to their lives and the lives of their children, especially after they have tried to leave the batterer. The reasons for staying also include the following:[26]

+ Fear of not getting custody of their children
+ Financial dependence
+ Feeling of responsibility for keeping the relationship together
+ Lack of support from family and friends

Many battered women remain in the abusive relationship because they believe the situation is inescapable or is part of their lot in life. They typically feel helpless about changing their lives and fear that any action they take will contribute to more violence. These fears are justified.[18]

Women have been thought to be culpable in their own violence; this implies that violence is more likely to occur in those situations where wives outshine their husbands in some presumably important way. Thus, to gain back a measure of self-respect, these husbands must batter their resourceful wives. However, women typically do not have more resources than men have in terms of income, education, or nearly any other valued resource imaginable that would account for the significant number of battered women.[18] In families where wives do earn higher salaries than their husbands, there is no evidence that family violence is any greater than in families where the husbands earn more than the wives.

Women who leave a battering relationship often mention that they had been close to another individual who gave them information and support, including an employee assistance program at their workplace.[5] This suggests that employers should respond to the needs of battered individuals, an issue to which we now turn.

## DOMESTIC VIOLENCE AS A WORKPLACE CONCERN

Jennifer Swanberg and T. K. Logan[1] recently asked women the following questions about ways in which domestic violence spills over into the workplace:

- How has domestic violence affected your job or your ability to find a job?
- Have you informed your employer about your situation? Why or why not?
- Have you informed co-workers about your situation? Why or why not?
- What supports, if any, has someone at your workplace offered you?
- How have the supports affected you and your life on the job?

Like other researchers, Swanberg and Logan[1] found that male abusers interfered with women's employment before work, during work, and after work. For example, prework tactics prevented 56 percent of the women in their study from going to work. Women reported being physically restrained, beaten, being refused the use of the car in order to get to work, and having their clothes cut up by the abuser. The majority of these women reported experiencing these forms of abuse at least once a week. Similar results were obtained by Kara Wettersten and her colleagues,[27] who interviewed employed women who were living in a battered women's shelter.

Women in the study by Swanberg and Logan[1] also reported that abusers interfered with their work responsibilities. Abusers showed up at work, harassed them over the phone, harassed their supervisors, and stalked them at work. According to one woman:

I was working at a restaurant and he showed up outside and just started beating on the back door. We had closed up and we were cleaning up for inspection and stuff and the manager come and told me that he was out there. I of course went outside I cold see that he was drunk and he was very angry ... he saw me talking with someone ... he started throwing me around the parking lot and they called the law and I got fired.

All the women described these experiences as frightening because the behavior on the part of the male abuser was unpredictable. For example:

I was the food stamp caseworker; it was the best money I ever made. He would pop up from nowhere, if I was gone too long [from my chair] he'd know it and then the phone calls would start from the outside phone booth. I had no idea how he knew my every move. If I stayed too late at work, the phone calls would start from home. The unpredictability was most stressful.... I was afraid I'd lose my job.

Among the women in this study, 46 percent informed their supervisors or managers about the domestic violence they were experiencing. This means that 54 percent of the women decided not to disclose this information. In addition, 43 percent of the women informed one of their co-workers about their being battered; 57 percent decided not to do so. Women who did inform their supervisor or co-workers also reported receiving support from these individuals. They received assistance with having their phone calls screened and physical protection from their batterer.

Women who decided not to disclose the battering chose this option because they feared they would lose their job, were ashamed of being battered, and wanted to handle their situation independently. We note that even the women who had indicated they received support from their employer and co-workers did resign eventually because of safety reasons, being forced by their abuser to stop working, and/or being too "upset and stressed" to continue to be employed.

These findings are similar to those obtained by Susan Lloyd and Nina Taluc.[28] They studied women in a low-income area of Chicago. Lloyd and Taluc asked women about their experiences with being battered. Of the 824 women in their sample, 18 percent said they had been physically assaulted, 11.9 percent had incurred more severe violence at the hand of their mate or spouse, and 40.3 percent said they had been coerced and threatened by their mate or spouse. In addition, 28.4 percent had experienced abuse at the criminal assault level. These women reported experiencing unemployment, emotional and physical health problems, and higher welfare rates than women who did not experience domestic violence.

## EMPLOYER SUPPORT

Could Barbara Cavalier's death and the death of her co-worker have been prevented? What kinds of support can employers offer to battered victims? Earlier in this book, we discussed the fact that workplace violence and aggression are significant sources of stress in the work environment and as such impact personal, health, social, work-related, and management aspects of the whole workforce. Employers must address domestic violence in the workplace since it poses a threat not only to the victim but to the safety of co-workers, vendors, and clients. Research indicates that battering annually costs employers more than $200 million in reduced worker productivity, increased turnover, and absenteeism. In addition, approximately 25 percent of women who visit emergency rooms are battered women. They incur more than $70 million in hospital bills annually. These realities demand that employers take remedial and educational steps to deal with domestic violence and its impact on the workplace.

Prevention strategies at the organizational level should include an explicit policy statement, investigatory procedures for handling complaints, and training programs for the entire workplace including the company's policy and procedures, so that employees know their rights and responsibilities.[29] A sample policy on domestic violence as a workplace concern is presented at the end of this chapter.

In addition, the Occupational Safety and Health Administration (OSHA)[30] recommends that a company train a threat assessment team, whose task it is to assist in dealing with workplace violence, and also in handling domestic violence. The responsibilities of the threat assessment team include assessing the vulnerability of the company to violence and serving as advocates for victims, including victims of domestic violence that has carried over into the workplace. The team should include representatives from senior management, employee assistance, security, and human resources staff.

OSHA has made it a requirement of employers to report illnesses and injuries stemming from domestic violence in the workplace.[30] OSHA has asserted that some types of domestic violence in the workplace may be prevented by security measures. Thus, information about these injuries and illnesses is relevant and must be included in workplace violence statistics.

Employers can also assist victims of domestic violence by developing a personalized safety plan for them.[30] This plan can include the following:

+ Include the workplace in the restraining order for the victim. Provide of the restraining order to the employee's supervisor, the employee's human resources representative, and security.
+ Save any threatening e-mail and/or voicemail messages.
+ Identify the parking arrangements; have security escort the employee to his or her car.
+ Remove the employee's name and phone number from automated phone directories.
+ Rotate the employee's work site or assignment if such a change would increase the employee's safety at the workplace.

Employees should decide what is needed in their plan since they are most familiar with their abusers. In addition, the company should maintain communication with the employee during that person's absence. The company must maintain the confidentiality of the employee's whereabouts. A sample personalized safety plan is presented at the end of this chapter.

Recommendations for additional preventative measures include the following:

+ Posting phone numbers of the following at worksites:

    Employee assistance program
    Security department
    National Domestic Violence Hotline number
    Local domestic violence resources
    Information on obtaining orders of protection
    List of certified batterers' intervention programs

+ Developing policies and other educational materials in languages spoken by employees
+ Modifying any human resource policies that negatively impact victims of domestic violence
+ Collaborating with domestic violence services available in the community

In addition to developing and enforcing effective policies and procedures and training programs on workplace violence, employers can partner with employee assistance programs (EAPs) in dealing with workplace violence.[30] For example, they may help employees to develop a sense of trust and safety in their current environment. Employee assistance programs can also help women employees foster relationships with appropriate, nonviolent male role models. Further, these programs can help employees counter any sense of guilt about having caused the violence and/or not being able to prevent the abuse. Trained counselors can offer several treatment modalities for employees, including cognitive and behavioral techniques to deal with specific problem behaviors, such as aggression. They can offer play assessment and therapy to encourage preschool children to express their feelings about the trauma; individual counseling for children, including specific strategies for creating a better understanding of their reaction to the abuse and their preparation for future violence; information about shelters and employee-children support groups. These services can be integrated with other community agencies. It is vital for agencies to work together, since women's economic independence plays a key role in their transition to leaving a violent relationship.

We return to this issue of the effective management of workplace violence in chapter 7.

## Sample Policy on Domestic Violence as a Workplace Concern

The employees of _____ must be able to work in an atmosphere of mutual respect and trust. As a place of work, _____ should be free of violence and all forms of intimidation and exploitation. _____ is concerned about and committed to our employees' safety and health. The company refuses to tolerate violence in our workplace.

_____ has issued a policy prohibiting violence in the workplace. We have zero tolerance for workplace violence.

_____ will also make every effort to prevent violent acts in this workplace perpetrated by spouses, mates, or lovers. The company is committed to dealing with domestic violence as a workplace issue. _____ has zero tolerance for domestic violence.

### Domestic Violence: Definition

Domestic violence—also referred to as battering, spouse abuse, spousal assault, and intimate partner abuse—is a global health problem. This victimization is defined as violence between adults who are intimates, regardless of their marital status, living arrangements, or sexual orientations. Such violence includes throwing, shoving, and slapping as well as beatings, forced sex, threats with a deadly weapon, and homicide.

### Domestic Violence: Myths and Realities

Myth: Domestic violence affects only a small percentage of employees.

Reality: Approximately 5 million employees are battered each year in the United States. Domestic violence is the leading cause of injury and workplace death for women in the United States.

Myth: People must enjoy the battering since they rarely leave the abusive relationship.

Reality: Very often victims of battering do leave the relationship. Women and men remain in a battering relationship not because they are masochistic, but for several well-founded reasons, e.g.,

- Threats to their lives and those of their children, especially after they have tried to leave the batterer
- Fear of not getting custody of their children
- Financial dependence
- Feeling of responsibility for keeping the relationship together
- Lack of support from family and friends

Myth: Individuals who batter their partners do so because they are under a great deal of stress, including the stress resulting from being unemployed.

Reality: Stress does not cause individuals to batter their partners. Society condones partner abuse. In addition, individuals who batter learn they can achieve their goals through the use of force without facing consequences.

Myth: Children are not affected by watching their parents in a battering relationship.

Reality: Children are often in the middle of domestic violence. They may be abused by the violent parent. Children may also grow up to repeat the behavior patterns they witnessed in their parents.

Myth: There are no long-term consequences of battering.

Reality: There are significant long-term consequences of battering, including depression, anger, fear, anxiety, irritability, loss of self-esteem, feelings of humiliation and alienation, and a sense of vulnerability.

Myth: Domestic violence occurs only in poor and minority families.

Reality: Domestic violence occurs in all socioeconomic classes and all racial and ethnic groups.

### Threat Assessment Team

_____ has established a Threat Assessment Team to assist with dealing with workplace violence. The duties of the Threat Assessment Team members include assessing the vulnerability of the company to domestic violence and serving as advocates for victims of workplace violence, including domestic violence that has carried over into the workplace.

All of the members of the Threat Assessment Team have received specialized training in workplace violence issues, including domestic violence as a workplace concern.

### Services Offered by _____ for Employees who are Victims of Domestic Violence

_____ will offer the following services for our employees who are victims of domestic violence:

- Provide receptionists and the building security officer with a photograph and a description of the batterer
- Screen the employee's visitors

- Screen the employee's calls
- Accompany the employee to her/his car
- Permit the employee to park close to the office building
- When there is a restraining order, the Vice President will send a formal notification to the batterer indicating that his/her presence on the company premises will result in arrest
- Provide referrals for individual counseling

### Sample Personalized Safety Plan

Name: _____
Date Completed: _____

1. I can inform my immediate supervisor, security, human resources and ____ at work that I am a victim of domestic violence.
2. I can ask _____ to help me screen my telephone calls at work.
3. When leaving work, I can walk with _____ to my car or the bus stop. I can park my car where I will feel safest getting in and out of the car.
4. If I have a problem while driving home I can _____ .
5. If I use public transit, I can _____ .
6. I can go to different grocery stores and shopping malls to conduct my business and shop at hours that are different from those I kept when residing with my battering partner.
7. I can use a different bank and go at hours that are different from those I kept when residing with my battering partner.
8. I can use _____ as my code word to alert my co-workers when I am in danger so they will call for help.

### Important Telephone Numbers

Police: 911 and _____
Domestic Violence Program: _____
District Attorney's Office: _____
My Supervisor's Home Phone Number: _____
Cell Phone Number: _____
My Clergy Contact's Phone Number: _____
Domestic Violence Shelter: _____
Human Resources Phone Number: _____
Security's Phone Number: _____
Other: _____

## RESOURCES

Graham-Bermann, S. A., & Edelson, J. (Eds.). (2001). *Domestic violence in the lives of children: The future of research, intervention, and social policy.* Washington, DC: American Psychological Association.

Lloyd, S. (1997). The effects of domestic violence on women's employment. *Law and Poverty, 19,* 139–167.

Sokoloff, N., & Pratt, C. (Eds.). (2005). *Domestic violence at the margins: Readings on race, class, gender and culture.* New Brunswick, NJ: Rutgers University Press.

Swanberg, J., & Logan, T. (2005). Domestic violence and employment: A qualitative study. *Journal of Occupational Psychology, 10,* 3–17.

Walker, L. (1999). Psychology and domestic violence around the world. *American Psychologist, 54,* 21–29.

## Associations Dealing with Intimate Partner Violence

American Domestic Violence Crisis Line
3300 NW 185th St., Suite 133
Portland, OR 97229
http://www.awoscentral.com

British Columbia Institute Against Family Violence
409 Granville Street, Suite 551
Vancouver, BC V6C IT2, Canada
http://www.bcifv.org

Canadian National Clearinghouse on Family Violence
1907D1 Tunney's Pasture
Ottawa, ON K1A 1B4, Canada
http://www.hc-sc.gc.ca/hppb/family violence

Domestic Violence Clearinghouse and Legal Hotline
PO Box 3198
Honolulu, HI 96801
http://www.stoptheviolence.org

International Society for Prevention of Child Abuse and Neglect
25W. 560 Geneva Rd., Suite L2C
Carol Stream, IL 60188
http://www.ispcan.org

National Clearinghouse on Child Abuse and Neglect
U.S. Department of Health and Human Services
1250 Maryland Ave, SW
Washington, DC 20024
703.385.7565

National Coalition Against Domestic Violence
PO Box 34103
Washington, DC 20043

Violence Against Women Office
U.S. Department of Justice
10th Street and Constitution Avenue, NW
Washington, DC 20530

# CHAPTER 7

# Managing Violence, Aggression, and Other Abusive Behaviors in the Workplace

The main goal of the future is to stop violence. The world is addicted to it.
—Bill Cosby

Opinions founded on prejudice are always sustained with the greatest of violence.
—Francis Jeffrey

The only thing that's been a worse flop than the organization of non-violence has been the organization of violence.
—Joan Baez

Those who make peaceful revolution impossible will make violent revolution inevitable.
—John F. Kennedy

The right things to do are those that keep our violence in abeyance; the wrong things are those that bring it to the fore.
—Robert J. Sawyer

## Questions for Reflection

+ What steps do you believe employers should take in preventing and dealing with workplace violence?
+ Who is the person at your job charged with dealing with workplace violence?

+ Does your employer insist on employees wearing identification badges while on the premises?
+ Have you received a copy of your company's policy on workplace violence? What is contained in this policy?
+ Have you experienced workplace violence? What did your employer do right in dealing with this violence? What do you believe your employer should have done differently?

---

*In August 1986, Patrick Sherrill, a U.S. postal employee in Edmond, Oklahoma, received a poor performance appraisal from his supervisor. Subsequently, he stole weapons from a National Guard armory and went to his workplace where he opened fire, killing 14 of his co-workers and injuring six more.*

*In June 2005, David Wilhelm entered the EPAC plastics plant in Savoy, Texas, and killed his estranged wife and her male co-worker, Felipe de Leon, before shooting himself. The Wilhelms were in the process of divorcing.*

*In March 1998 at the Connecticut Lottery Corporation, Matthew Beck, 35, an accountant involved in a pay dispute, fatally shot the president of the organization and three of his supervisors before killing himself.*

It seems inevitable that most organizations will have to deal with some form of abusive behavior frequently if not daily. Fortunately, the most extreme forms of violence and aggression described in the above cases are relatively rare, but that does not mean there are no other significant problems. Furthermore, there are many forms of abusive behavior that do not reach the threshold of violence, and some may be difficult even to identify as aggressive. However, we now know that when we are dealing with workplace mistreatment of any sort it must be taken seriously and dealt with as effectively and completely as possible.

## CREATING A WORKPLACE VIOLENCE POLICY

Everyone in the organization has an interest in keeping the workplace as safe and free from abuse, violence, and retaliation as is possible.[1] For any organization, the best way to management workplace aggression and violence is prevention. The Occupational Safety and Health Administration (OSHA)[2] relies on Section 5 (a) (1) of the OSA Act, also referred to as the "General Duty Clause." This clause requires employers to "furnish to each … employee employment and a place of employment which are free from recognized hazards that are causing or are likely to cause death or serious physical harm to … employees." Section 5 (a) (2) states that employers are required to "comply with occupational safety and health standards promulgated under this Act." While prevention is expensive, it is clearly not as expensive as the cost of an unsafe and dangerous work environment.

D. Chappell and V. DeMartino[3] suggested that when developing programs to manage workplace violence, a number of responses must be considered:

+ Preventive: The employer must look for and deal with the causes of violence and aggression.
+ Targeted: Not all types of violence can be handled in the same way. Select the type you need to deal with and handle it directly.
+ Multiple: Combinations of responses are needed to deal with complex problems.
+ Immediate: A potentially dangerous situation must be responded to without delay.
+ Participatory: Any program or intervention should be based upon involvement and participation by relevant employees.
+ Long-term: Problems not dealt with today are bigger problems for tomorrow.

E. A. Rugala and A. R. Isaacs[4] also reported that any preventive programs to be developed must be legal, must be nondiscriminatory, and must protect the rights of all involved, including job applicants. The principles of a good prevention program include the following:

+ It must be supported from the top of the organization.
+ There is no "one size fits all" strategy.
+ The plan should be proactive and not reactive.
+ The plan should take into account the workplace culture.
+ Planning and responding calls for expertise from a number of perspectives.
+ Managers should take an active role in communicating the workplace prevention policies to the employees.
+ The plan should be practiced.
+ The plan should be reevaluated, rethought, and revised as necessary.

In following these principles and OSHA's guidelines, we recommend that organizations should have the following in place: an effective and enforced policy statement, an effective and enforced investigatory procedure, and training in workplace violence awareness and the company's policy and procedures for all members of the organization. We discuss each of these in the next section.

## Policy Statement

One measure that is essential to any organization trying to find strategies for managing workplace violence and aggression is to have a workplace violence prevention policy statement.[1] A good policy requires more than a statement of compliance with OSHA guidelines. It must be designed both to prevent workplace violence and to remedy any violations that might occur.

Several important elements must be included in an effective policy.[2] An organization that pays attention to each of these will be doing what is necessary to put together a program that will meet the needs of employees and managers and will stand the ultimate test in court, if that should ever become necessary.

An overriding consideration for any workplace violence policy is whether it sets a tone of appropriate seriousness and concern for the employees' rights. The statement of policy needs to specify clearly and directly the types of behaviors that are not acceptable in the workplace, and the potential consequences of such behaviors. It is also important to specify the full range of unacceptable behaviors from the most to the least extreme. The standards, expectations, and consequences should be clear, public, and made available to every employee.[2]

The following components of effective workplace violence policies have been identified by OSHA:[2]

- Employees should be educated about the hazards in the workplace.
- Workers should not be put or put themselves in a situation where they are at risk for violence.
- Employees who work with the public should be trained to deal with potentially violent situations and learn how to handle themselves in such situations.
- Potentially violent clients should be managed appropriately and staff should be made aware of the clients who are at risk for violence.
- Back-up support should be available to those employees who want it.
- Employees should be encouraged to report all events, near misses, and threats.
- All events should be investigated.
- Management should provide assistance for anyone who wants to press charges legally.
- Management must apply rules consistently and fairly.

By defining the types of behavior and threatening language that are forbidden, organizations expect to make the workplace safer. Most certainly, any organization should have clear guidelines for unacceptable behavior, particularly when it involves aggression or abuse. However, there are some potential problems with zero-tolerance policies in general. First, simply issuing a piece of paper does not in itself make things safer; it may contribute to an illusion of security that does not really exist. Further, if there are problems in the workplace, they may simply be covered up or ignored by the "zero-tolerance policy." Also, this type of policy might actually violate labor contracts that specify "progressive discipline." One of the problems that can emerge with zero tolerance policies is that they can go too far in defining threatening behavior and open the door for some managers to use the policies unfairly to harass or abuse employees. Finally, when these types of policies allow for immediate dismissal for threatening language they rarely take into account some of the cultural differences found in a diverse workforce. Thus, an employee might be dismissed for a simple misunderstanding that is misperceived by a manager who is not familiar with intercultural differences in communication.

A sample policy statement is presented at the end of this chapter.

## Investigatory Procedures

Effective investigatory procedures include the following, as is illustrated in the sample policy:[5]

+ A plan for controlling hazards and preventing violence from occurring
+ Methods for assessing hazards
+ A strategy for handling violence when it happens
+ Union or worker involvement in the development and implementation of a violence prevention program
+ Management commitment to the full implementation of the plan

We offer recommendations and cautionary notes with regard to the following common elements of most workplace violence investigative procedures:[5]

### Profiles

Profiling can be very problematic and potentially illegal depending upon how it is used. In the hands of trained professionals who look for more than age, sex, and race, profiles have a role, perhaps, but certainly not in businesses or organizations where profiles might be used to discriminate against a group of people who happen to fit some type of template. It is one thing to single out a person because he or she shows the types of behaviors that are considered to be high risk, but quite another to pay particular attention to someone because of his or her demographic characteristics.

### Psychological Tests

It is extremely difficult to predict who will become violent or when violence will be committed. Most often the violence will occur far beyond the predictive scope of the tests. Certainly there are effective uses for psychological tests in the workplace, but predicting violence is not one of them.

### Preemployment Screening

Factors such as a history of violence or threatening behaviors and a history of drug or alcohol abuse bear further examination. It is essential that any preemployment screening should be legal and fair, and should contain background and personal histories, personal interviews (with more than one person when possible), background and reference checks, and drug test results where appropriate. In this type of situation it is important that any irregularities in information or conflicting impressions be followed up and evaluated. On the other hand, protecting applicant rights is also protecting the rights of others in the workplace too, so these must be respected as well.

Preemployment screening will help to identify problematic behaviors and conditions that might lead to violence. It is also necessary to be aware of workplace or social conditions that place people at risk, and assess for those as well. The workplace must be inspected by someone with expertise in the area. A safety survey should be conducted; organizational safety and incident records should be analyzed as well. By reviewing prior incidents we can find out if a problem exists and how serious it is, and even whether management is aware that a problem exists. We can also try to determine if there are trends in a particular department or work area, at a certain time, in different jobs, or under a particular supervisor or manager. These findings will go a long way to help determine if there is a problem, where there is a problem, and under what conditions the problem exists. These facts will help determine what kinds of steps can be taken to minimize the impact of a violent incident or hopefully even to prevent it from emerging.

## Threat Assessment Teams

OSHA recommends the use of threat assessment or crisis intervention teams that are trained to receive, evaluate, and respond to threats in the workplace.[2] Serious problems can result if the team is not adequately trained and does not implement policies properly. For example, these teams might intervene inappropriately in a situation and actually make it worse, possibly endangering themselves or others. Further, these teams can become very abusive and even feared by workers as some type of "secret police" spying on people to try to get them into trouble. These teams must involve a variety of members from management and labor and should also include a trained mental health professional. The range of responsibilities for these teams must be clearly spelled out to avoid the possibility that they might overstep their bounds or abuse the rights of others.

The following steps can be implemented to insure that these teams are effective and appropriate: (1) an inclusive group of employees to represent the organization should be selected; and (2) training that offers legal, management, and psychological perspectives should be provided to the team on a periodic basis.

## Policies that Exclude the Union

If workplace violence prevention programs have any chance of being effective, they must involve the employees in the planning and implementation at every stage of the program. This strategy will give the program more credibility. In addition, employees will anticipate problems and add elements to the program that management and consultants might not have included.

### One-Sided Management Policies

If policies are adopted that do not apply equally to management and employees, there will be problems. For example, if zero-tolerance policies serve to get employees dismissed for behavior that is acceptable for managers, then one would expect some serious disgruntlement from employees. To make sure that these policies are recognized and enforced equally and fairly, they must apply to all employees including supervisors and managers.

### Failure to Manage

The best programs are worthless if they are not implemented.[5] Making sure that people are informed and well trained is essential, but it is also necessary that the people who are responsible for implementing the programs do so appropriately and fairly.

## Training Programs

Managers should have the training and support to implement prevention programs. If managers are afraid to carry out their responsibilities, either because they are unsure as to what they should do or because they fear they will not be supported by upper management, the violence prevention programs will not work.

Training programs should basically contain the following:[7]

+ The workplace violence prevention policy including reporting requirements
+ Risk factors that can cause or contribute to threats and violence
+ Early recognition of warning signs of problematic behavior
+ Where appropriate, ways of preventing and diffusing volatile situations or aggressive behavior
+ Information on cultural diversity to develop sensitivity to racial and ethnic issues and differences
+ A standard response action plan for violent situations, including the availability of assistance, response to alarm systems, and communication procedures
+ The location and operation of safety devices such as alarm systems, along with required maintenance schedules and procedures
+ Ways to protect oneself and co-workers including the use of a "buddy system"
+ Policies and procedures for reporting and record keeping
+ Policies and procedures for obtaining medical care, counseling, workers' compensation, or legal assistance after a violent episode or injury

Not only will training very probably make the workplace safer, but it will also make employees feel more confident in their ability to deal with potentially dangerous situations, and it will make them more confident that their management is also trained and equipped to deal with problematic situations. Minimally, employees should know how and what to report, what procedures to follow, and what numbers to call if there is a problem (see below).

---

### Interview with James Amanatides

Workplace violence is never anything an employer can predict happening with employees. It doesn't happen as often as you would like to believe but we all hear news reports when it does happen. It is important that companies have training programs established so that employees can recognize the warning signs and know what to do if they see the warning signs in a fellow employee. You cannot impress upon them enough the importance of reporting the behavior to a supervisor or manager so the individual can be spoken with directly. These are situations that cannot be ignored or delayed.

Not only is it important to be able to recognize the signs, but your training program should include what to do in case it happens. Employees and their supervisors should know who will call the police, who will call 911, who will greet the authorities and/or ambulance when they arrive, etc. Your employee handbook should also make it very clear that you have zero tolerance for this and that it will lead to immediate termination. The company policy also needs to be part of the training program. Supervisors and managers also need to be involved in the training so that they, too, can be aware of what can happen. Supervisors and managers can become targets if an employee is being disciplined, terminated, or fails to receive a raise or promotion. You cannot predict what will occur and sometimes it may be necessary to have another supervisor or manager present during these situations.

---

James Amanatides, SPHR, is the human resources (HR) manager at Portola Packaging in Clifton Park, NY. He manages the HR function for a 100-person manufacturing facility, which produces tamper-evident plastic closures. Portola has three other U.S. plants plus an international presence. Jim has over 20 years of progressive HR experience and has held positions at Albany Medical Center and Garden Way, Inc. He is a graduate of SUNY–Empire State College in New York.

---

In addition to employee training, if an organization is serious about developing programs to control and prevent violence and aggression, training of supervisors and managers is essential. This can be part of the general training or separate from it, but at some point, some of the supervisor-specific elements need to be identified and included as part of targeted training. Thus, some organizations might choose to do general training for all personnel, and then have additional targeted training for employees, managers, or others. Some components of effective training programs for supervisors include the following:

+ Ways to encourage employees to report problems
+ Skills in behaving compassionately and supportively to employees who report problems
+ Skills in taking disciplinary action
+ Skills in handling crises
+ Basic emergency procedures
+ Ways to ensure that appropriate preemployment screening has been done

Organizations must also train their incident response team or threat assessment team to deal with situations as they emerge or after they have occurred. These teams should receive very detailed and continuing training. Their training must include everything taught to the other groups, but it should include other elements as well:[2]

+ These teams need to be professionally competent and know what to do and when to call for help.
+ All members need to know the other team members and their individual jobs very well.
+ They should role-play and practice a wide variety of potential problem situations.
+ They should have frequent meetings and ongoing training.

## MANAGING VIOLENCE AND AGGRESSION WHEN IT OCCURS

As simple as this may sound, it is not always easy to know what to do or when to intervene when a potentially difficult situation emerges. Clearly, when something arises that might be of concern, three basic steps need to be taken: first, identify the threat; second, deal with the threat; third, report the incident.[2] However, most organizations are not even clear as to what constitutes a threat unless it is an extreme situation. According to Rugala and Isaacs[4] a threat is "Any verbal or physical conduct that threatens property or personal safety or that reasonably could be interpreted as an intent to cause harm." Thus, we should be concerned with physical *and* verbal behavior that conveys "an intent to cause harm." Of course, it is never easy to know what someone else's intentions are, but this definition specifies that anything that "reasonably could be interpreted" as intended to cause harm should be of concern. This eliminates a frequent defense: "I didn't mean anything by that—they are just overly sensitive." However, even an excellent definition does not solve the problem of what to do when violence or aggression is observed. Cal/OSHA has identified guidelines as to what to do to deal early with potential problems:[6]

+ Know your rights and responsibilities.
+ Intervene promptly.

+ Be clear about the facts of the problem as you see them.
+ Ask people who are involved to describe their perceptions of the problem.
+ Set clear expectations.
+ Assess additional needed resources and get outside help as needed.
+ Follow up.

This deceptively simple list of things to do can be a huge advantage if people know what to do and when to do it. Simply having the right people trained and ready to respond can keep a difficult situation from becoming a tragedy. Consider the following example:

An employee complains that a co-worker frequently talks to himself, and it is bothersome and distracting. The complaining employee says that she has frequently asked her co-worker not to talk out loud unless he is in a conversation with her, but he continues to do so. The employee feels that her co-worker is doing this intentionally to irritate her, and says it is because she does not talk to him socially and has refused his offers of going out on a date. When asked about this by his manager, the co-worker simply says that he has tried to be friendly to her in the past, but that she is very cold and unfriendly and is very uptight and rigid. He acknowledges that he does at times talk to himself when he is working, to help him clarify his ideas, and nobody else has ever complained about it. Is this truly passive-aggressive behavior? Clearly, without a confession it is hard to prove. However, the manager can look at the consequences and deal with the behavior on that basis. He can point out that the other person has requested that her co-worker should not talk to himself around her because it is distracting and interferes with her work. At this point, the manager can tell the offending employee that productivity is a management issue and can say, "I do not know if you are doing this casually or intentionally or if you are trying to annoy her or not. However, I do know that your job doesn't require that you talk to yourself, and when you do this it interferes with the productivity of another employee. Thus, there is no basis for disciplinary action at this point, but if this behavior continues, then it will be my conclusion that you are doing this intentionally and against my explicit orders, and this will be something that will result in a disciplinary action."

This example shows how a manager can deal with passive-aggressive behavior directly without having to get into a debate regarding intentions and misinterpretations.

The American Federation of State, County, and Municipal Employees (AFSCME)[5] suggested a number of steps that should be followed after a violent event has occurred. Of course, any injuries must be treated appropriately and referred to medical personnel outside the workplace if additional care is needed. It is also vitally important to recognize and deal with the possibility of psychological harm being caused to the victim and any others who are party to or affected by the violent event. Thus, caring for the physical and psychological/emotional needs of anyone affected by the violent event(s) must be the highest priority.

Whenever a violent event occurs there must be a post-incident report. AFSCME[5] suggested that the following be included in such a report:

+ Were any injuries or harm done?
+ Where did the event(s) occur?
+ Was the worker alone?
+ Was a security guard on duty?

    + If "yes," was the guard notified?
    + If "yes," did the guard respond?

+ At what time did the violent event occur?
+ Who was the perpetrator of the event?
+ Were there threats before the incident?
+ Did the affected worker report being threatened or harassed?

    + If so, what was done?

+ What type of weapon was used?

    + How did the perpetrator get the weapon
    + How did the weapon get into the work environment?

+ Had the affected worker ever received training on workplace violence?
+ What were the main factors contributing to the incident?
+ What could have prevented the incident?

The most important thing about a post-incident report is that it is essential to get all of the important information recorded as soon as possible. The half-life for information following such an event is very short. That means that the accuracy and completeness of information following a violent incident drops off dramatically as time passes. People who are responsible for collecting this type of information must be adequately trained and must be available when these events occur.[1]

Further, critical incident debriefing must occur for all staff. This will help the parties to start to deal with and heal from the events that have occurred. It is very important to recognize that often people will not follow through with reporting violent and aggressive events in the workplace because they fear reprisals and do not expect to be supported. These factors will interfere with the collection of information and will also make the effects of the violence even worse than they might be.

Finally, appropriate counseling must be provided for all employees (this includes managers as well). It is vitally important that those providing the counseling be trained to deal with victims of violence. If this expertise is not found in-house (e.g., in an employee assistance program), then it must be obtained from the outside. This kind of help is essential and will reduce problems like turnover, absenteeism, decreased performance, poor morale, and further conflict. These types of problems are frequently found following violence in the workplace, but they can be minimized by appropriate intervention.

Organizations that conscientiously take these suggestions to heart and try to implement them will find that they are able to avoid and/or manage violent and aggressive events more effectively.[1] The best programs in the world will not reduce the risk to zero, but the better programs will keep the risks within acceptable bounds.

Finally, Cal/OSHA[6] provided a very helpful series of steps to follow in order to reduce the potential risk of a difficult situation, and to minimize the damage if violence erupts. This is very complete and thorough, and it bears a full description and discussion.

*Step One:* **General Response to Disruptive Behavior (No Threats or Weapons).**

1. Respond quietly and calmly.
2. Do not take the behavior personally.
3. Ask questions.
4. Consider offering an apology—even if you have done nothing wrong.
5. Summarize what you hear the individual saying—focus on areas of agreement.
6. If this does not stop the disruption, determine whether the person seems dangerous.
7. If you think the person is upset but not a threat, then set limits and seek assistance as needed.

*Step Two:* **If Step One Is Ineffective and the Person *Does Not* Seem Dangerous.**

1. Calmly and firmly set limits.
2. Ask the individual to stop the behavior and warn that official action might be taken.
3. If the disruption continues despite the warning, then say that disciplinary or legal action will be taken.
4. If the individual refuses to leave after being directed to do so, inform the individual that this refusal is a violation subject to discipline, and so forth.

*Step Three:* **If Step One Is Ineffective and the Individual *Does* Seem Dangerous.**

1. If possible, find a quiet, safe place to talk, but do not isolate yourself.
2. Use a calm, nonconfrontational approach to diffuse the situation.
3. *Never* touch the individual yourself or try to remove him/her from the area.
4. Set limits to indicate the behavior needed to deal with the concern.
5. Signal for assistance (use a prearranged signal).
6. Do not mention discipline or the police if you fear an angry or violent response.
7. If the situation escalates, find a way to excuse yourself, leave the area, and get help.

*If an Emergency Occurs:*

1. Call the appropriate officials.
2. Call the police.
3. *Do not* intervene physically.
4. Get yourself and others to safety ASAP.
5. If possible, keep a line to the police open until they arrive.

*Post-Incident Response:*

1. Follow up with all involved and affected people.
2. Provide support and care for those who need it.
3. Make appropriate referrals for those who require them.
4. Send the necessary reports to the appropriate offices and agencies.

## ADDITIONAL PREVENTION STRATEGIES

When we think about developing prevention programs we need to be mindful of the need to look at prevention more broadly. In the public health arena, we conceptualize prevention in terms of primary, secondary, and tertiary types of prevention.[8] This approach is certainly applicable in the workplace. For example, primary prevention has to do with dealing with the whole relevant population of people who may be involved and reducing the risks for everyone. Therefore, general policies and education programs for employees, customers, vendors, and management would be an example of primary prevention. Secondary prevention works with people who are at high risk either for being victims or for being perpetrators and targeting them for more intensive training or preventive measures. For example, a person working at night in a convenience store is in a higher risk situation, and should probably have more in the way of training and other resources to keep him or her safe. Or perhaps we have an employee with a history of violence and alcohol problems. It would be appropriate to require this employee to participate in some additional training or programs to keep him or her and the people around him or her safer.

Finally, tertiary prevention deals with people after a problem has emerged, and it is intended to keep the problem from getting worse or leading to more chronic difficulties. Thus, working with victims of violence or abuse, providing supportive and counseling services as needed, is one way of minimizing future problems. In addition, if a person has committed some act that has created problems and is still a part of the organization, providing education, training, and even counseling for that person would probably help reduce the risk of future problems. This may also salvage a potentially valuable employee before he or she does something that demands dismissal.

Security measures should include a weapons policy and employee ID badges for all personnel. When appropriate, organizations should also consider on-site guard services and/or coded card keys for access. Guards or trained personnel in larger organizations should also be present to register, badge, and direct people to the proper location.

Organizations should bear in mind that many of the techniques used for other health and safety issues can be used for the prevention or control of violence and aggression. The idea of modifying the work environment to make it safer is an "engineering solution"[8] that should also be assessed and considered. Such solutions can be very helpful. Some examples of engineering controls are:

+ Controlling or limiting access to work areas, especially after dark
+ Installing locks on doors that lead to "staff only" areas like break or lunch rooms
+ Using personnel and visitors' badges, and limiting the personal information on the badges
+ Creating good, clear escape routes
+ Where appropriate, installing deep counters and bullet- or shatterproof glass between customers and staff
+ Locking up medical tools or medications and any sharp tools
+ Using metal detectors
+ Providing mobile phones or pagers and personal alarms or portable panic buttons for field personnel
+ Increasing security controls and especially in the evening and early morning

Clearly, these engineering suggestions are not intended for all or even most organizations, but they give some examples of how these types of interventions can be used to make the work environment as safe as possible. Obviously, customer or client safety, comfort, convenience, and needs are important as well, as are the potential costs and maintenance expenses for such solutions. Recognizing that one violent incident can have terribly costly and harmful results, these and any other solutions need to be examined with a view to the whole situation. Proposed solutions should not cause more problems than they prevent.

One other approach to the prevention of workplace violence is the use of alternative dispute resolution techniques (ADR):[9]

*Ombudsperson:* This is an individual who has the authority to intervene and hopefully resolve or minimize a potential problem and keep it from getting worse. The use of a variety of approaches such as problem solving and suggesting options can often be very helpful. Usually, these people cannot *impose* solutions, but if their suggestions are accepted and acted upon, then official intervention may not be needed.

*Facilitation:* In this approach an individual who is not part of the conflict may get involved to help resolve the dispute. This individual does not engage in dealing with issues related to the content of the difficulties but does help manage the processes so that he/she can help the conflicted parties move toward a resolution.

*Mediation:* This is a step above facilitation. It also involves a person who is independent of the conflict but assists in arriving at a solution. However, in mediation the person may offer options and suggestions as well as facilitate the deliberations. Mediators may work with the different parties separately or together, and while they do not usually have the authority to impose solutions, they are involved with the content of the dispute as well as the process of resolution.

*Interest-based Problem Solving:* This technique works to arrive at solutions while improving relationships at the same time. This approach has been used successfully in labor negotiations, and it tries to define arguments in terms of issues while avoiding making the disputes more personalized.

*Peer Review:* In some organizations, peer panels may become involved to counsel and to help resolve disputes and suggest remedies. Depending upon the organization, this panel may have some authority to impose its judgment.

Finally, any good program *must* have an evaluation component, which should include the following elements:[7]

+ Establishing a uniform reporting system for incidents of harassment, bullying, threats, and other inappropriate behavior, and also a regular review of reports of incidents at work
+ Measuring the frequency and severity of workplace violence in order to determine if prevention programs are having the desired effect
+ Analyzing trends and rates in violence-related injuries, the amount of lost work, and so forth
+ Surveying employees before and after making job or worksite changes or installing security measures or new systems, to determine their effectiveness
+ Keeping abreast of new strategies for dealing with workplace violence as they become available.

Certainly, precautions like these can be very helpful and possibly help avoid potential crises or difficult situations. AFSCME[5] suggested additional measures that can be implemented by organizations to protect employees:

+ Using a "buddy system" or other type of backup when entering a dangerous situation
+ Having a daily work plan and making sure someone knows where every employee is at all times
+ Providing a communication device like a cell phone or walkie-talkie
+ Providing a portable "panic button" for each employee
+ Considering personal protection devices when appropriate
+ Keeping vehicles well maintained and always keeping them locked
+ Providing handheld alarms

+ Discouraging employees from carrying anything that could be used as a weapon (pen, knife, etc.)
+ Being aware that uniforms are not always welcome in some areas
+ Ensuring that health care workers never wear medical dress or carry a medical bag in public places, as these workers may be a target because people think they have drugs
+ Establishing a relationship with local police
+ Offering free legal assistance to people who want to press charges
+ Giving employees the option not to enter a dangerous situation without backup

Preventing violence demands that all members of the workplace community should in concert. For example, the responsibilities of human resources staff include the following:

+ Facilitating supervisory training
+ Addressing employee problems promptly
+ Assisting supervisors to determine what course of administrative action is appropriate given the situation
+ Investigating complaints of workplace violence

The responsibilities of an employee assistance program counselor include the following:

+ Providing short-term counseling to employees and managers
+ Providing referrals for counseling outside the organization
+ Training employees in dealing with angry co-workers, vendors, and customers through conflict resolution and communication skills
+ Consulting with the threat assessment team
+ Training supervisors to deal with problems as they arise without diagnosing the employee

The responsibilities of unions include the following:

+ Supporting the workplace violence policy and contract language on prevention strategies
+ Consulting with the threat assessment team
+ Consulting with the employee assistance program
+ Collaborating with all levels of management to ensure employees are up to date on the organization's workplace violence policy and procedures
+ Providing training on workplace violence and domestic violence as a workplace concern as part of steward/delegate training

Security staff play important roles in prevention strategies, including the following:

+ Working with personnel to improve the security level of the buildings, grounds, and parking lots

+ Serving as the organization's security experts, alerting management to the risk of violence, to problems identified by the threat assessment team, and to technologies to deal with problems
+ Serving as the liaison with local law enforcement

In general, good sense, careful planning, support, and appropriate responses will go a long way toward preventing problems in the workplace. Conflict is normal and healthy and does not have to lead to violence or aggression.[10] However, when conflict arises it must be addressed promptly and not avoided or suppressed. Management must work to facilitate a workplace environment that promotes healthy and positive methods of dealing with problems, methods that do not disrupt the workplace or scare or bother others. Certainly, working with staff at all levels to improve conflict management skills is appropriate, as well as setting and enforcing clear standards of conduct. Finally, providing help (e.g., mediation or counseling) to address conflicts early can be beneficial.[11]

Also, every organization must have emergency action plans that are well known and practiced. These plans must have the following:

+ Procedures for calling for help
+ Procedures for calling for medical assistance
+ Procedures for notifying the proper authorities
+ Emergency escape procedures and routes for every person and for every place in the organization
+ Safe places to go inside and outside the building if problems occur
+ Procedures for securing the area after a violent event
+ Procedures for accounting for all employees after a violent event
+ Identification of personnel with the training needed to perform medical or rescue duties
+ Training for employees on how to deal with violence and how to use the emergency action plan[5]

When specific types of threats emerge it is important to be able to respond to them quickly and also appropriately. For example, it is not uncommon for organizations to receive bomb threats, and fortunately all but a very small number are crank calls or harassment threats.[5] However, particularly in this age of terrorism, bomb threats can never be ignored and must always be taken seriously. Whenever such a threat occurs, the facility must be evacuated and the appropriate authorities (e.g., police, bomb squad) must be notified. All employees, but especially receptionists and secretaries who may be on the front line, must be trained as to what they should do if such a threat is made. Further, there should be clear procedures to follow when there is a bomb threat or a suspicious phone call, letter, or note. It should always be made clear that employees who do not have appropriate training should *never* search for a bomb or try to disarm one on their own. All employees should be trained to be aware of suspicious packages or parcels, and if one is observed, they should know exactly what to do and whom to call.

We also suggest that organizations that do not have bomb threat procedures and are not sure what to do should have the local police suggest procedures and review the process when it is in place.

Preventing and managing all forms of aggressive and abusive behavior is the business and responsibility of everyone in an organization. Training programs and management strategies should start with this fundamental point in mind.[12] To the extent that the workplace provides good, responsive/responsible programs and processes, and has a workforce and management that is trained and committed to keeping the workplace safe and healthy, then we can expect workplace violence to be far less of an issue than it is today.

### Policy on Workplace Violence

Managers and employees of _____ must be able to work in an atmosphere of mutual respect and trust. As a place of work, _____ should be free of violence and all forms of intimidation and exploitation. _____ is concerned about and committed to our employees' safety and health. We refuse to tolerate violence in our workplace and will make every effort to prevent violent incidents in this workplace. All employees at all levels must refrain from engaging in violence in the workplace and will be held responsible for insuring that _____ is free from violence. Any employee who engages in such behavior will be subject to disciplinary procedures.

_____ has issued a separate policy statement dealing with domestic violence as a workplace issue.

### What Is Workplace Violence?

Workplace violence includes, but is not limited to, verbal threats, nonverbal threats, pushing, shoving, hitting, assault, stalking, murder, and related actions. These behaviors constitute workplace violence whether they are committed by people who are in a supervisory position or by co-workers, vendors, clients, or visitors. And these behaviors constitute workplace violence if they occur between employees of the same sex or between employees of the opposite sex.

### Threat Assessment Team

_____ has established a Threat Assessment Team to assist with dealing with workplace violence. The duties of the Threat Assessment Team members include assessing the vulnerability of _____ to workplace violence and serving as advocates for victims of workplace violence, as explained below.

All of the members of the Threat Assessment Team have received specialized training in workplace violence issues, including prevention.

### Reporting Workplace Violence

_____ requires prompt and accurate reporting of all violent incidents whether or not physical injury has occurred. Any employee who has a complaint of workplace violence is encouraged to report such conduct to the Threat Assessment Team so that the complaint may be investigated and resolved promptly.

All complaints of workplace violence will be investigated by the Human Resources Director.

Complainants and those against whom complaints have been filed will not be expected to meet together to discuss the resolution of the complaint.

Employees who file a complaint of workplace violence may do so orally and/or in writing.

### Investigating Complaints of Workplace Violence

The Human Resources Director will investigate the complaint of workplace violence. The investigation will be limited to what is necessary to resolve the complaint. If it appears necessary for the Human Resources Director to speak to any individuals other than those involved in the complaint, he/she will do so only after informing the complainant and the person against whom the complaint is made.

The Human Resources Director will endeavor to investigate all complaints of workplace violence expeditiously and professionally. In addition, he/she will make every attempt to maintain the information provided to him/her in the complaint and investigation process as confidentially as possible. If warranted, the Human Resources Director will work with local police officials in resolving the complaint of workplace violence.

Complaints will be investigated in the following manner by the Human Resources Director:

1. Upon receipt of a written complaint, the Human Resources Director will ask the individual if he/she has any witnesses he/she would like to be interviewed on his/her behalf. Individuals will complete a form providing names of witnesses as well as the issues that the witnesses may address. Complainants will provide the Human Resources Director with a signed statement giving him/her permission to contact these witnesses.
2. The Human Resources Director will immediately forward a copy of the complaint, along with a copy of _____'s Workplace Violence Policy Statement and Procedures, to the individual complained against and request a meeting with this individual within three business days.
3. During the meeting with the respondent, the Human Resources Director will ask the individual if he/she has any witnesses he/she would like to be interviewed on his/her behalf. Individuals will complete a form providing names of witnesses as well as the issues that the witnesses may address. Complainants will provide the Human Resources Director with a signed statement giving him/her permission to contact these witnesses.

4. Names or other identifying features of witnesses on behalf of the complainant and respondent will not be made known to the opposing party. This will help ensure participation by witnesses in the investigation.

5. The Human Resources Director will investigate all complaints expeditiously and professionally. To the maximum extent possible, the investigation will be completed within two weeks from the time the formal investigation is initiated. The Human Resources Director will also maintain the information provided to him/her in the complaint and investigation process as confidential. Parties to the complaint will be asked to sign a "Confidentiality" form in which they state they will keep the complaint and complaint resolution confidential. They will also be asked to sign a form indicating they will not retaliate against any party to the complaint.

6. A safe environment will be set up for the complainant, respondent, and witnesses to discuss their perspectives without the fear of being ridiculed or judged.

7. No conclusions about the veracity of the complaint will be made until the investigation is completed.

8. All documents presented by the parties to the complaint will be reviewed by the Human Resources Director. Documents include, but are not limited to, letters and notes.

9. Following the completion of an investigation, the Human Resources Director will make one of the following determinations:

+ Sustain the Complaint: A finding of violence has been made and recommendations for corrective action will be identified, including reprimands, relief from specific duties, transfer, or dismissal.
+ Not Sustain the Complaint: A finding of no violence has been made.
+ Insufficient Information: Insufficient information exists on which to make a determination. All parties will be reinvestigated.

10. Following any determination and recommendations for corrective action, the Human Resources Director will issue a written decision with findings to the President. The President will correspond with the complainant and the person complained against, informing them of the findings of the investigation and recommendations for corrective action. The President will make appropriate statements of apology to individuals involved in the complaint.

11. If complainants are not satisfied with internal procedures, they may seek redress through other sources, for example, the Office for Civil Rights, the U.S. Department of Education, OSHA.

There will be no retaliation against employees for reporting workplace violence or assisting the investigators in the investigation of a complaint. Any retaliation against an employee member is subject to disciplinary action.

If after investigating any complaint of workplace violence it is discovered that the complaint is not bona fide or that an employee has provided false information regarding the complaint, the employee may be subject to disciplinary action.

### Inspection of Company for Workplace Violence

The Threat Assessment Team will review previous incidents of violence at _____.
The team will review existing records, identifying patterns that may indicate the causes and severity of assault incidents as well as identifying changes necessary to correct these hazards. In addition, the Threat Assessment Team will inspect _____ and evaluate the work tasks of all employees to determine the presence of hazards, conditions, operations, and other situations that might place employees at risk of workplace violence. Periodic inspections will be performed every three months, on the first Friday of the month.

The Threat Assessment Team will also survey employees at _____ to identify and confirm the need for improved security measures. These surveys will be conducted once a year.

### Training

_____ will provide training on workplace violence annually to all employees.

## RESOURCES

Baron, S. (2001). *Violence in the workplace: A prevention and management guide for businesses.* New York: Pathfinder.

Kelloway, K., Barling, J., & Hurrell, J. (Eds.). (2006). Handbook of workplace violence. New York: Sage.

Schell, B., & Lantergne, N. (2000). *Stalking, harassment, and murder in the workplace: Guidelines for protection and prevention.* Westport, CT: Quorum.

# Notes

## PREFACE

1.  See U.S. Department of Labor, Occupational Safety and Health Administration (OSHA), http://www.osha.gov.

2.  J. Budd, R. Avvey, and P. Lawless, "Correlates and Consequences of Workplace Violence," *Journal of Occupational Health Psychology* 1 (1996): 197–210.

3.  G. VandenBos and E. Bulatao, eds., *Violence on the Job: Identifying Risks and Developing Solutions* (Washington, DC: American Psychological Association, 1996).

4.  J. Barling, "Prediction, Experience, and Consequences of Violence," in *Violence on the Job: Identifying Risks and Developing Solutions*, ed. G. VandenBos and E. Bulatao (Washington, DC: American Psychological Association, 1996).

5.  C. Rayner and H. Hoel, "A Summary Review of Literature Relating to Workplace Bullying," *Journal of Community and Applied Social Psychology* 7 (1997): 181–191.

6.  See National Institute for Occupational Safety and Health (NIOSH), http://www.niosh.gov.

7.  See Society for Human Resource Management (SHRM), http://www.shrm.org.

8.  K. Rogers and E. K. Kelloway, "Violence at Work: Personal and Organizational Outcomes," *Journal of Occupational Health Psychology* 3 (1997): 63–71.

9.  J. Barling, S. Bluen, and R. Fain, "Psychological Functioning Following an Acute Disaster," *Journal of Applied Psychology* 72 (1987): 683–690.

10. S. Hershcovis and J. Barling, "Preventing Insider-Initiated Workplace Violence," in *Handbook of Workplace Violence*, ed. E. K. Kelloway, J. Barling, and J. Hurrell (New York: Sage, 2006).

11. E. K. Kelloway, J. Barling, and J. Hurrell, *Handbook of Workplace Violence* (New York: Sage, 2006).

12. R. Nydegger, M. Paludi, E. DeSouza, and C. Paludi, "Incivility, Sexual Harassment and Violence in the Workplace," in *Gender, Race, and Ethnicity in the Workplace*, ed. M. Karsten (Westport, CT: Praeger, 2006).

## CHAPTER 1

1. National Occupational Health and Safety Commission, "Program One Report: Occupational Violence" (presented at 51st Meeting of NOHSC, 10 March 1999).

2. Occupational Safety and Health Administration, *OSHA Guidelines for Preventing Workplace Violence for Health Care and Social Service Workers*, OSHA3148–01R 2000, http://www.osha.gov, 2004.

3. U.S. Department of Justice, *Violence and Theft in the Workplace*, NJC-148199, (Annapolis Junction, MD: Bureau of Justice Statistics, 1994).

4. E. DeSouza and J. Solberg, "Incidence and Dimensions of Sexual Harassment Across Cultures," in *Academic and Workplace Sexual Harassment: A Handbook of Cultural, Social Science, Management, and Legal Perspectives*, ed. M. Paludi and C. Paludi (Westport, CT: Praeger, 2003).

5. U.S. Department of Justice, Bureau of Justice Statistics, "About 2 Million People Attacked or Threatened in the Workplace Every Year," http://www.ojp.usdoj.gov/bjs/pub/press/wv96.pr.

6. L. Cortina and V. Magley, "Raising Voice, Risking Retaliation: Events Following Interpersonal Mistreatment in the Workplace," *Journal of Occupational Health Psychology* 4 (2003): 247–265.

7. J. Greenberg and R. Baron, *Behavior in Organizations*, 6th ed. (Upper Saddle River, NJ: Prentice-Hall, 1997).

8. U.S. Department of Justice, 2003.

9. S. Barrett, "Protecting against Workplace Violence: Protection for Workers To Be Given by the Federal, State, and Local Governments," *Public Management* 79 (1997): 9.

10. J. Barab, "Public Employees as a Group at Risk for Violence," *Occupational Medicine* 11 (1996): 257–267.

11. J. Swanberg and T. Logan, "Domestic Violence and Employment: A Qualitative Study," *Journal of Occupational Health Psychology* 10 (2005): 3–17.

12. M. Lerner, *The Belief in a Just World: A Fundamental Delusion* (New York: Plenum, 1980).

13. C. Peek-Asa, C. Runyan, and C. Zwerling, "The Role of Surveillance and Evaluation Research in the Reduction of Violence against Workers," *American Journal of Preventive Medicine* 20 (2001): 141–148.

14. R. A. Baron and J. H. Neumann, "Workplace Violence and Workplace Aggression: Evidence on Their Relative Frequency and Potential Causes," *Aggressive Behavior* 22 (1996): 161–173.

15. H. Hoel and K. Sparks, "The Cost of Violence/Stress at Work and the Benefits of a Violence/Stress-Free Working Environment," Institute of Science and Technology, University of Manchester, UK, 2001.

16. R. Nydegger, M. Paludi, E. DeSouza, and C. Paludi, "Incivility, Sexual Harassment and Violence in the Workplace," in *Gender, Race, and Ethnicity in the Workplace*, ed. M. Karsten (Westport, CT: Praeger, 2006).

17. J. Greenberg and R. Baron, *Behavior in Organizations*, 6th ed. (Upper Saddle River, NJ: Prentice-Hall, 1997).

18. J. Warren, D. Brown, S. Hurt, S. Cook, and W. Branson, "The Organizational Context of Non-lethal Workplace Violence: Its Interpersonal, Temporal, and Spatial Correlates," *Journal of Occupational and Environmental Medicine* 41 (1999): 567–581.

19. L. Walker, "Psychology and Domestic Violence around the World," *American Psychologist* 54 (1999): 21–29.

20. D. Chappell and V. DeMartino, *Violence at Work* (Geneva, Switzerland: International Labour Office, 1998).

21. United Nations Committee on the Elimination of Discrimination against Women, 1998.

22. See National Institute for Occupational Safety and Health (NIOSH), http://www.niosh.gov.

23. W. I. Thomas, *The Unadjusted Girl* (Boston: Little, Brown, 1923).

24. J. Bruner and R. Taguiri, "Person Perception," in *Handbook of Social Psychology*, ed. G. Lindzey (Reading, MA: Addison Wesley, 1954).

25. R. Merton, "The Self-Fulfilling Prophecy," *Antioch Review* 8 (1948): 193–210.

26. E. Jones, D. Kanouse, H. Kelley, R. Nisbett, S. Valins, and B. Weiner, *Attribution: Perceiving the Causes of Behavior* (Morristown, NJ: General Learning Press, 1972).

27. E. Jones and V. Harris, "The Attribution of Attitudes," *Journal of Experimental Social Psychology* 3 (1967): 1–24.

28. L. Babcock and G. Loewenstein, "Explaining Bargaining Impasse: The Role of Self-Serving Biases," *Journal of Economic Perspectives* 11 (1997).

## CHAPTER 2

1. Workplace Violence Headquarters, "The Realities and Options," 2005, http://www.workplace-violence-hq.com.

2. R. Wynne, N. Clarkin, T. Cox, and A. Griffiths, *Guidance on the Prevention of Violence at Work*, DG-V, Ref. CE/V1–4/97 (Brussels: European Commission, 1997).

3. T. H. Shea, "Workplace Violence: Turning Down the Heat," *Workplace Violence Prevention Report* 6 (2000).

4. National Occupational Health and Safety Commission, "Program One Report: Occupational Violence" (presented at 51st Meeting of NOHSC, 10 March 1999).

5. R. Nydegger, M. Paludi, E. DeSouza, and C. Paludi, "Incivility, Sexual Harassment and Violence in the Workplace," in *Gender, Race, and Ethnicity in the Workplace*, ed. M. Karsten (Westport, CT: Praeger, 2006).

6 California Occupational Safety and Health Administration (Cal/OSHA), *Guidelines for Workplace Security*, http://www.hr.ucdavis.edu, 1994.

7. R. Denenberry and M. Braverman, *The Violence Prone Workplace* (Ithaca, NY: Cornell University Press, 1999).

8. R. Baron and J. Neumann, "Workplace Violence and Workplace Aggression: Evidence on Their Relative Frequency and Potential Causes," *Aggressive Behavior* 22 (1996): 161–173.

9. H. Hoel and K. Sparks, "The Cost of Violence/Stress at Work and the Benefits of a Violence/Stress-Free Working Environment," Institute of Science and Technology, University of Manchester, UK, 2001.

10. L. Lapierre, P. Spector, and J. Leck, "Sexual versus Nonsexual Workplace Aggression and Victims' Overall Job Satisfaction: A Meta-Analysis," *Journal of Occupational Health Psychology* 10 (2005): 155–169.

11. L. Price Spratlen, "Interpersonal Conflict Which Includes Mistreatment in a University Workplace," *Violence and Victims* 10 (1995): 285–297.

12. L. Keashly, "Emotional Abuse in the Workplace: Conceptual and Empirical Issues," *Journal of Emotional Abuse* 1 (1998): 85–117.

13. R. Nydegger, "Violence, Aggression and Passive-Aggression in the Workplace," *Management Development Forum* 3 (2000): 89–96.

14. R. A. Baron and J. H. Neumann, "Workplace Aggression: The Iceberg beneath the Tip of Workplace Violence," *Public Administration Quarterly* 21 (1998): 446.

15. Canada Safety Council, "Bullying in the Workplace," 2005, http://www.safety-council.org/info/OSH/bullies.html.

16. P.A.J. Waddington, D. Badger, and R. Bull, "Appraising the Inclusive Definition of Workplace Violence," *British Journal of Criminology* 45 (2005): 141–164.

## CHAPTER 3

1. J. Bowman and C. Zigmond, "State Government Responses to Workplace Violence," *Public Personnel Management* 26 (1997): 289.

2. National Safe Workplace Institute, "Workplace Violence and Behavior Letter," no. 1 (1994).

3. J. A. Kinney, *Preventing Violence at Work* (Englewood, NJ: Prentice-Hall, 1995).

4. Teamsters, "Safety and Health Facts," 2005, http://www.ibtsafety@teamsters.org.

5. J. Mattman and S. Kanfer, eds., *The Complete Workplace Violence Prevention Manual: Volume I* (Costa Mesa, CA: James Publishing, 1998).

6. D. Chappell and V. DeMartino, *Violence at Work* (Geneva, Switzerland: International Labour Office, 1998).

7. G. Toscano and W. Weber, "Violence in the Workplace," 1995, Bureau of Labor Statistics, http://www.bls.gov/osh/cfar0005.pdf.

8. Workplace Violence Headquarters, "The Realities and Options" 2005, http://www.workplace-violence-hq.com.

9. J. Greenberg and R. Baron, *Behavior in Organizations*, 6th ed. (Upper Saddle River, NJ: Prentice-Hall, 1997).

10. G. Warchol, "Workplace Violence, 1992–1996," National Crime Victimization Survey (1998).

11. R. B. Flannery, *Violence in the Workplace* (New York: Crossroad Publishing Company, 1995).

12. T. Feldman and P. Johnson, "Workplace Violence: A New Form of Lethal Aggression," in *Lethal Violence*, ed. H. Hall (Kamuela, HI: Pacific Institute for the Study of Conflict and Aggression, 1996).

13. California Occupational Safety and Health Administration (Cal/OSHA), *Guidelines for Workplace Security*, http://www.hr.ucdavis.edu, 1994.

14. National Crime Victimization Survey, "Violence in the Workplace: 1993–1999," *Bureau of Justice Statistics Special Report* (2001).

15. K. Schaffer, C. Casteel, and J. Kraus, "A Case-Site/Control/Site Study of Workplace Violent Injury," *Journal of Occupational and Environmental Medicine* 44 (2002): 1018–1026; S. Perrot and E. K. Kelloway, "Workplace Violence in the Police," in *Handbook of Workplace Violence*, ed. E. K. Kelloway, J. Barling, and J. Harrell (New York: Sage, 2006); M. Lanza, "Violence in Nursing," in *Handbook of Workplace Violence*, ed. E. K. Kelloway, J. Barling, and J. Harrell (New York: Sage, 2006).

16. E. Bulatao and G.. VandenBos, "Workplace Violence: Its Scope and the Issues," in *Violence on the Job: Identifying Risks and Developing Solutions*, ed. G. VandenBos and E. Bulatao (Washington, DC: American Psychological Association, 1996).

17. Teamsters, "Safety and Health Facts," (2005), http://www.ibtsafety@teamsters.org.

18. J. Warren, D. Brown, S. Hurt, S. Cook, and W. Branson, "The Organizational Context of Non-lethal Workplace Violence: Its Interpersonal, Temporal, and Spatial Correlates," *Journal of Occupational and Environmental Medicine* 41 (1999): 567–581.

19. National Center for Victims of Crimes, "Workplace Violence: Employee Information," 2005, http://www.ncvc.org.

20. C. Mayhew and D. Chappell, "The Occupational Violence Experience of Some Australian Health Workers: An Exploratory Study," *Journal of Occupational Health Safety* 19 (2003): 3–43; T. Glomb and L. Cortina, "The Experience of Victims: Using Theories of Traumatic and Chronic Stress to Understand Individual Outcomes of Workplace Abuse," in *Handbook of Workplace Violence*, ed. E. K. Kelloway, J. Barling, and J. Harrell (New York: Sage, 2006).

21. H. Resnick, S. Galea, D. Kilpatrick, and D. Vlahor, "Research on Trauma and PTSD in the Aftermath of 9/11," *PTSD Research Quarterly* 15 (2004): 1–6.

22. T. Barnett-Queen and L. H. Bergman, "Response to Traumatic Event Crucial in Preventing Lasting Consequences," *Occupational Health and Safety*, 53 (2001): 53–55.

23. American Federation of State, County, and Municipal Employees (AFSCME), "Workplace Violence," 2005, http://www.afscme.org/health/faq-viol.htm.

24. J. Barling, A. G. Rogers, and E. Kelloway, "Behind Closed Doors: In-Home Workers' Experience of Sexual Harassment and Workplace Violence," *Journal of Occupational Health Psychology* 6 (2001): 225–269.

25. L. Lapierre, P. Spector, and J. Leck, "Sexual Versus Non-Sexual Workplace Aggression and Victims' Overall Job Satisfaction: A Meta-analysis," *Journal of Occupational and Health Psychology* 10 (2005): 155–169.

26. R. W. Griffith, P. Hom, and S. Gaertner, "A Meta-Analysis of Antecedents and Correlates of Employee Turnover: Update, Moderator Tests and Research Implications for the Next Millennium," *Journal of Management* 26 (2000): 463–488.

27. R. A. Baron, *Violence in the Workplace: A Prevention and Management Guide for Business* (Ventura, CA: 1993).

## CHAPTER 4

1. K. T. Liou, "Understanding Violence in the Workplace: Social and Managerial Perspectives," 1999, http://www.pamij.com/99_4_3_Liou.html.

2. D. Chappell and V. DeMartino, *Violence at Work* (Geneva, Switzerland: International Labour Office, 1998).

3. S. C. Douglas and M. J. Martinko, "Exploring the Role of Individual Differences in the Prediction of Workplace Aggression," *Journal of Applied Psychology* 86 (2001): 547–559.

4. T. Harris, *Applied Organizational Communications: Perspectives, Principles and Pragmatics* (Hillsdale, NJ: Lawrence Erlbaum, 1993).

5. R. A. Baron and D. R. Richardson, *Human Aggression*, 2nd ed. (New York: Plenum, 1994).

6. D. Holmes and M. Will, "Expression of Interpersonal Aggression by Angered and Non-angered Persons with Type A and Type B Behavior Patterns," *Journal of Personality and Social Psychology* 40 (1985): 723–727.

7. K. Dodge, J. Price, J. Bachorowski, and J. Neumann, "Personal Attributional Bias in Severely Aggressive Adolescents," *Journal of Abnormal Psychology* 99 (1990): 385–392.

8. R. Nydegger, "Violence, Aggression and Passive-Aggression in the Workplace," *Management Development Forum* 3 (2000): 89–96.

9. J. Neumann and R. Baron, "Workplace Violence and Workplace Aggression: Evidence Concerning Specific Forms, Potential Causes, and Preferred Targets," *Journal of Management* 24 (1998): 391–419.

10. P. E. Spector, "The Contribution of Personality Traits, Negative Affectivity, Locus of Control and Type A to the Subsequent Reports of Job Stressors and Job Strains," *Journal of Occupational and Organizational Psychology* 67 (1994): 1–12.

11. L. Berkowitz, *Aggression: Its Causes, Consequences, and Control* (Philadelphia: Temple University Press, 1993).

12. J. Swanberg and T. Logan, "Domestic Violence and Employment: A Qualitative Study," *Journal of Occupational Health Psychology* 10 (2005): 3–17.

13. L. Greenberg and J. Barling, "Predicting Employee Aggression against Coworkers, Subordinates and Supervisors: The Role of Person Behaviors and Perceived Workplace Factors," *Journal of Organizational Behavior* 20 (1999): 897–913.

14. N. Stuckles and R. Goranson, "The Vengeance Scale: Development of a Measure of Attitudes toward Revenge," *Journal of Social Behavior and Personality* 7(7) (1992): 25–42.

15. H. Hoel and K. Sparks, "The Cost of Violence/Stress at Work and the Benefits of a Violence/Stress-Free Working Environment," Institute of Science and Technology, University of Manchester, UK, 2001.

16. J. Dollard, L. Doob, N. Miller, O. Mowrer, and R. Sears, *Frustration and Aggression* (New Haven, CT: Yale University Press, 1939).

17. L. Lapierre, P. Spector, and J. Leck, "Sexual Versus Nonsexual Workplace Aggression and Victims' Overall Job Satisfaction: A Meta-Analysis," *Journal of Occupational Health Psychology* 10 (2005): 155–169.

18. R. A. Clay, "Securing the Workplace: Are Our Fears Misplaced?" *Monitors on Psychology* 31 (2000): 1–8.

19. D. W. Myers, "The Mythical World of Workplace Violence—Or Is It?" *Business Horizons* 39 (1995): 31–36.

20. L. H. Pastor, "Initial Assessment and Intervention Strategies to Reduce Workplace Violence," *American Family Physicians* 52 (1995): 1987.

21. California Occupational Safety and Health Administration (Cal/OSHA), *Guidelines for Workplace Security*, http://www.hr.ucdavis.edu, 1994.

22. C. Mayhew and D. Chappell, "The Occupational Violence Experience of Some Australian Health Workers: An Exploratory Study," *Journal of Occupational Health Safety* 19 (2003): 3–43.

23. C. Gray, "Reducing the Risk of Workplace Violence," *Foundry Management and Technology* 126 (1998): 74.

24. J. Brockner, S. Grover, T. Reed, and R. DeWitt, "Layoffs, Job Insecurity, and Survivors' Work Effort: Evidence of an Inverted U Relationship," *Academy of Management Journal* 35 (1992): 413–426.

25. M. J. Martinko and K. L. Zellars, "Toward a Theory of Workplace Violence and Aggression: A Cognitive Appraisal Perspective," in *Dysfunctional Behavior in Organizations: Violent and Deviant Behavior*, ed. R. Griffin, A. O'Leary-Kelly, and J. Collins (Stamford, CT: JAI Press, 1998).

26. B. Sharif, "Understanding and Managing Job Stress: A Vital Dimension of Workplace Violence Prevention," *International Electronic Journal of Health Education* 3 (2000): 107–116.

27. K. R. Pelletier, *Healthy People in Unhealthy Places: Stress and Fitness at Work* (New York: Dell, 1985).

28. J. Barling, "Prediction, Experience, and Consequences of Violence, in *Violence on the Job: Identifying Risks and Developing Solutions*, ed. G. VandenBos and E. Bulatao (Washington, DC: American Psychological Association, 1996).

29. See National Institute for Occupational Safety and Health (NIOSH), http://www.niosh.gov

30. Health 24.com, "Are You a Problem Boss?" 2005, http://www.health24.com/women/general/711–733–1500,25199.asp.

31. TTG Consultants, "Preventing Workplace Terrorism and Other Violence," 2005, http://www.ttgconsultants.com/preventing-workplace-violence.

32. Teamsters, "Safety and Health Facts," 2005, http://www.ibtsafety@teamsters.org.

33. J. Brockner, S. Grover, T. Reed, and R. DeWitt, "Layoffs, Job Insecurity, and Survivors' Work Effort: Evidence of an Inverted U Relationship," *Academy of Management Journal* 35 (1992): 413–426.

34. R. Baron and J. Neumann, "Workplace Violence and Workplace Aggression: Evidence on their Relative Frequency and Potential Causes," *Aggressive Behavior* 22 (1996): 161–173.

35. D. P. Skarlicki and R. Folger, "Retaliation in the Workplace: The Roles of Distributive, Procedural, and Interactional Justice," *Journal of Applied Psychology* 82 (1997): 434–443.

36. W. Hepworth and A. Towler, "The Effects of Individual Differences and Charismatic Leadership on Workplace Aggression," *Journal of Occupational Health Psychology* 9 (2004): 176–185.

37. American Federation of State, County, and Municipal Employees (AFSCME), "Workplace Violence," 2005, http://www.afscme.org/health/faq-viol.htm.

38. A. Bandura, D. Ross, and S. A. Ross, "Transmission of Aggression through Imitation of Aggressive Models," *Journal of Abnormal and Social Psychology* 63 (1961): 575–582.

39. L. R. Huesmann, J. Moise-Titus, C. Podolski, and L. Eron, "Longitudinal Relations between Children's Exposure to TV Violence and Their Aggressive and Violent Behavior in Young Adulthood: 1977–1992," *Developmental Psychology* 39 (2003): 201–221.

40. J. Cantor, *Mommy, I'm Scared! How TV and Movies Frighten Children and What We Can Do to Protect Them* (San Diego, CA: Harcourt Brace, 1998).

41. J. Johnson, P. Cohen, E. Smailes, S. Kasen, and J. Brook, "Television Viewing and Aggressive Behavior during Adolescence and Adulthood," *Science* 29 (2002): 2468–2471.

42. M. D. Slater, K. Henry, R. Swain, and J. Cardador, "Vulnerable Teens, Vulnerable Times," *Communication Research* 31 (2004): 642–668.

43. B. Bushman and C. Anderson, Media Violence and the American Public: Scientific Facts versus Media Misinformation," *American Psychologist* 56 (2001): 477–489.

44. M. Medved, "Hollywood's 3 Big Lies," *Reader's Digest* 147 (1995): 155–129.

45. M. B. Oliver, "Portrayals of Crime, Race, and Aggression in 'Reality Based' Police Shows: A Content Analysis," *Journal of Broadcasting and Electronic Media* 38 (1994): 179–192.

## CHAPTER 5

1. *Code of Federal Regulations*, volume 29, section 1604.11 (2000).

2. Equal Employment Opportunity Commission (EEOC), "Guidelines and Discrimination because of Sex," *Federal Register* 45 (1980): 74676–74677.

3. A. Levy and M. Paludi, *Workplace Sexual Harassment* (Upper Saddle River, NJ: Prentice-Hall, 2002).

4. M. Paludi and R. Barickman, *Education, Work, and Sexual Harassment* (Albany: State University of New York Press, 1998).

5. E. DeSouza and J. Solberg, "Incidence and Dimensions of Sexual Harassment Across Cultures," in *Academic and Workplace Sexual Harassment: A Handbook of Cultural, Social Science, Management, and Legal Perspectives*, ed. M. Paludi and C. Paludi (Westport, CT: Praeger, 2003).

6. L. Fitzgerald, "Sexual Harassment: The Definition and Measurement of a Construct," in *Sexual Harassment on College Campuses*, ed. M. Paludi (Albany: State University of New York Press, 1997).

7. U.S. Merit Systems Protection Board, *Sexual Harassment in the Federal Workplace: Is It a Problem?* (Washington, DC: U.S. Government Printing Office, 1981).

8. U.S. Merit Systems Protection Board, *Sexual Harassment in the Federal Government: An Update* (Washington, DC.: U.S. Government Printing Office, 1988).

9. M. Martindale, *Sexual Harassment in the Military: 1988* (Washington, DC: Manpower Data Center, Department of Defense, 1990).

10. L. Bastian, A. Lancaster, and H. Reyst, *The Department of Defense 1995 Sexual Harassment Survey* (Arlington, VA: Defense Manpower Data Center, 1996).

11. L. Fitzgerald, S. Shullman, N. Bailey, M. Richards, J. Swecher, Y. Gold, M. Ormerod, and L. Weitzman, "The Incidence and Dimensions of Sexual Harassment in Academia and the Workplace," *Journal of Vocational Behavior* 32 (1988): 152–167.

12. B. Gutek, *The Impact of Sexual Behavior and Harassment on Women, Men, and Organizations* (San Francisco, CA: Jossey Bass, 1985).

13. L. Fitzgerald, F. Drasgow, C. Hulin, M. Gelfand, and V. Magley, "The Antecedents and Consequences of Sexual Harassment in Organizations: A Test of an Integrated Model," *Journal of Applied Psychology* 82 (1997): 578–589.

14. Y. Gold, "The Sexualization of the Workplace: Sexual Harassment of Pink, White and Blue-Collar Workers" (paper presented at annual meeting, American Psychological Association, New York City, August 1997).

15. See Equal Employment Opportunity Commission (EEOC), http://www. eeoc.gov.

16. R. Barickman, M. Paludi, and V. Rabinowitz, "Sexual Harassment of Students? Victims of the College Experience," in *Victimization: An International Perspective*, ed. E. Viano (New York: Springer, 1992).

17. G. Gutek and B. Morash, "Sex Ratios, Sex-Role Spillover, and Sexual Harassment of Women at Work," *Journal of Social Issues* 38 (1982): 55–74.

18. L. Cortina and S. Wasti, "Profiles in Coping: Responses to Sexual Harassment across Persons, Organizations, and Culture," *Journal of Applied Psychology* 90 (2005): 182–192.

19. A. Barak, "Cross-Cultural Perspectives on Sexual harassment," in *Sexual Harassment: Theory, Research, and Treatment*, ed. W. O'Donohue (Boston, MA: Allyn and Bacon, 1997).

20. J. Gruber, K. Kauppinen, and M. Smith, "Sexual Harassment Types and Severity: Linking Research and Policy," in *Women and Work: Sexual Harassment in the Workplace*, ed. M. Stockdale (Thousand Oaks, CA: Sage, 1996).

21. L. Fitzgerald and S. Shullman, "Sexual Harassment: A Research Analysis and Agenda for the 90s," *Journal of Vocational Behavior* 42 (1993): 5–29.

22. B. Dansky and D. Kilpatrick, "Effects of Sexual Harassment," in *Sexual Harassment: Theory, Research, and Treatment*, ed. W. O'Donohue (Boston: Allyn and Bacon, 1997).

23. P. Lundberg-Love and S. Marmion, "Sexual Harassment in the Private Sector," in *Academic and Workplace Sexual Harassment: A Handbook of Cultural, Social Science, Management, and Legal Perspectives*, ed. M. Paludi and C. Paludi (Westport, CT: Praeger, 2003).

24. B. Gutek and M. Koss, "How Women Deal with Sexual Harassment and How Organizations Respond to Reporting," in *Sexual Harassment in the Workplace and Academia: Psychiatric Issues*, ed. D. Schrier (Washington, DC: American Psychiatric Press, 1996).

25. J. Gruber and L. Bjorn, "Women's Responses to Sexual Harassment: An Analysis of Sociocultural, Organizational, and Personal Resource Models," *Social Science Quarterly* 67 (1986): 814–826; S. Wasti and L. Cortina, "Coping in Context: Sociocultural Determinants of Responses to Sexual Harassment," *Journal of Personality and Social Psychology* 83 (2002): 394–405.

26. K. Hanisch and C. Hulin, "Job Attitudes and Organizational Withdrawal: An Examination of Retirement and Other Voluntary Withdrawal Behaviors," *Journal of Vocational Behavior* 37 (1990): 60–78.

27. J. Hamilton, S. Alagna, L. King, and C. Lloyd, "The Emotional Consequences of Gender-Based Abuse in the Workplace: New Counseling Programs for Sex Discrimination," *Women and Therapy* 6 (1987): 155–182.

28. J. Swanberg and T. Logan, "Domestic Violence and Employment: A Qualitative Study," *Journal of Occupational Health Psychology* 10 (2005): 3–17.

29. J. Barling, A. G. Rogers, and E. K. Kelloway, "Behind Closed Doors: In-Home Workers' Experience of Sexual Harassment and Workplace Violence," *Journal of Occupational Health Psychology* 6 (2001): 255–269.

30. L. Fitzgerald, Y. Gold, and K. Brock, "Responses to Victimization: Validation of an Objective Policy," *Journal of College Student Personnel* 27 (1990): 34–39.

31. A. Ormerod and Y. Gold, "Coping with Sexual Harassment: Internal and External Strategies for Coping with Stress" (paper presented at annual meeting, American Psychological Association, Bethesda, MD, March 1988).

32. M. Stites, "Consensual Relationships," in *Sexual Harassment on College Campuses: Abusing the Ivory Power*, ed. M. Paludi (Albany: State University of New York Press, 1996).

33. P. DeChiara, "The Need for Universities to Have Rules on Consensual Relationships between Faculty and Students," *Columbia Journal of Law and Social Problems* 21 (1988): 137–162.

34. S. R. Zalk, "Women Students' Assessment of Consensual Relationships with Their Professors: Ivory Power Reconsidered," in *Academic and Workplace Sexual Harassment: A Resource Manual*, ed. M. Paludi and R. Barickman (Albany: State University of New York Press, 1991).

35. L. Fitzgerald and A. Omerod, "Sexual Harassment in Academia and the Workplace," in *Psychology of Women: A Handbook of Issues and Theories*, ed. F. Denmark and M. Paludi (Westport, CT: Greenwood Press, 1993).

36. L. Fitzgerald and L. Weitzman, "Men Who Harass: Speculation and Data," in *Ivory Power*, ed. M. Paludi (Albany: State University of New York Press, 1990).

37. J. Doyle and M. Paludi, *Sex and Gender* (New York: McGraw Hill, 1997).

38. M. Paludi, "Ivory Power Revisited: Changed Individuals, Changed Campuses" (paper presented at Vermont Women in Higher Education Conference, Burlington, VT, November 1993).

39. S. Lim and L. Cortina, "Interpersonal Mistreatment in the Workplace: The Interface and Impact of General Incivility and Sexual Harassment," *Journal of Applied Psychology* 90 (2005): 483–496.

40. J. Wilson and G. Kelling, "Broken Windows: The Police and Neighborhood Safety," *Atlantic Monthly*, March 1982.

41. B. Sandler and M. Paludi, *Educator's Guide to Controlling Sexual Harassment* (Washington, DC: Thompson, 1992).

42. Equal Employment Opportunity Commission (EEOC), "Policy Guidance on Sexual Harassment," March 1990.

43. J. Salisbury and F. Jaffe, "Individual Training of Sexual Harassers," in *Sexual Harassment on College Campuses*, ed. M. Paludi (Albany: State University of New York Press, 1996).

44. C. Paludi and M. Paludi, "Developing and Enforcing Effective Policies, Procedures, and Training Programs for Educational Institutions and Businesses," in *Academic and Workplace Sexual Harassment: A Handbook of Cultural, Social Science, Management, and Legal Perspectives*, ed. M. Paludi and C. Paludi (Westport, CT: Praeger, 2003).

45. B. Gutek, "Sexual Harassment Policy Initiatives," in *Sexual Harassment: Theory, Research, and Practice*, ed. W. O'Donohue (Boston: Allyn and Bacon, 1997).

46. I. McQueen, "Investigating Sexual Harassment Allegations: The Employer's Challenge," in *Sexual Harassment: Theory, Research, and Treatment*, ed. W. O'Donohue (Boston: Allyn and Bacon, 1997).

## CHAPTER 6

1. J. Swanberg and T. Logan, "Domestic Violence and Employment: A Qualitative Study," *Journal of Occupational Health Psychology* 10 (2005): 3–17.

2. J. Swanberg, T. Logan, and C. Macke, "The Consequences of Partner Violence on Employment and the Workplace," in *Handbook of Workplace Violence*, ed. E. K. Kelloway, J. Barling, and J. Hurrell (New York: Sage, 2006).

3. D. Graham, E. Rawlings, and R. Rigsby, *Loving to Survive: Sexual Terror, Men's Violence, and Women's Lives* (New York: New York University Press, 1994).

4. D. Follingstad, B. Rutledge, E. Berg, E. Hause, and D. Polek, "The Role of Emotional Abuse in Physically Abusive Relationships," *Journal of Family Violence* 5 (1990): 107–120.

5. M. Paludi, "Ivory Power Revisited: Changed Individuals, Changed Campuses" (paper presented at Vermont Women in Higher Education Conference, Burlington, VT, November 1993).

6. K. Ryan, I. H. Frieze, and H. Sinclair, "Physical Violence in Dating Relationships," in *The Psychology of Sexual Victimization: A Handbook*, ed. M. Paludi (Westport, CT: Greenwood Press, 1999).

7. F. Gryl, S. Stith, and G. Bird, "Close Dating Relationships among College Students: Differences by Use of Violence and by Gender," *Journal of Social and Personal Relationships* 8 (1991): 243–264.

8. M. Strauss, R. Gelles, and C. Smith, *Physical Violence in American Families: Risk Factors and Adaptations to Violence* (New Brunswick, NJ: Transaction Publishers, 1990).

9. L. Walker, "Psychology and Domestic Violence around the World," *American Psychologist* 54 (1999): 21–29.

10. C. Tran and K. DesJardins, "Domestic Violence in Vietnamese Refugee and Korean Immigrant Communities," In *Relationships among Asian American Women*, ed. J. Chin (Washington DC: American Psychological Association, 2000).

11. J. Kozu, "Domestic Violence in Japan," *American Psychologist* 54 (1999): 50–54.

12. S. Horne, "Domestic Violence in Russia," *American Psychologist* 54 (1999): 55–61.

13. C. Antonopoulou, "Domestic Violence in Greece," *American Psychologist* 54 (1999): 63–64.

14. L. Heise, "Violence against Women: An Integrated, Ecological Framework," *Journal of Violence against Women* 4 (1998): 262–290.

15. M. Potoczniak, J. Murot, M. Crosbie-Burnett, and A. Potoczni, "Legal and Psychological Perspectives on Same-Sex Domestic Violence," *Journal of Family Psychology* 17 (2003): 252–259.

16. E. Pizzey, *Scream Quietly or the Neighbors Will Hear* (Berkeley Heights, NJ: Enslow Publishers, 1978).

17. L. Walker, *The Battered Woman* (New York: Harper and Row, 1979).

18. D. Graham and E. Rawlings, "Observers' Blaming of Battered Wives: Who, What, When and Why?" in *The Psychology of Sexual Victimization: A Handbook*, ed. M. Paludi (Westport, CT: Greenwood Press, 1999).

19. H. Hughes, S. Graham-Bermann, and G. Gruber, "Resilience in Children Exposed to Domestic Violence," *Domestic Violence and Children: The Future of Research, Intervention, and Social Policy*, ed. S. Graham-Bermann and J. Edleson (Washington, DC: American Psychological Association, 2001).

20. A. Levendosky, A. Huth-Bocks, D. Shapiro, and M. Sernel, "The Impact of Domestic Violence on the Maternal-Child Relationship and Preschool Children's Functioning," *Journal of Family Psychology* 17 (2003): 275–287.

21. S. Graham-Bermann and J. Seng, "Violence Exposure and Traumatic Stress Symptoms as Additional Predictors of Health Problems in High-Risk Children," *Journal of Pediatrics* 146 (2005): 349–354.

22. B. Rossman, "Long-Term Effects of Children's Exposure to Domestic Violence," in *Domestic Violence and Children: The Future of Research, Intervention, and Social Policy*, ed. S. Graham-Bermann and J. Edleson (Washington, DC: American Psychological Association, 2001).

23. W. McGuigan, S. Vuchinich, and C. Pratt, "Domestic Violence, Parents' View of Their Infant, and Risk for Child Abuse," *Journal of Family Psychology* 14 (2000): 613–624.

24. L. Friedman and S. Crouper, *The Cost of Domestic Violence: A Preliminary Investigation of the Financial Cost of Domestic Violence* (New York: Victim Services Agency, 1987).

25. S. Riger, C. Ahrens, and A. Blickenstaff, "Measuring Interference with Employment and Education Reported by Women with Abusive Partners: Preliminary Data," *Violence and Victims* 15 (2000): 161.

26. J. Pearson, N. Theonnes, and E. Griswold, "Child Support and Domestic Violence: The Victims Speak Out," *Violence against Women* 5 (1999): 427–448.

27. K. Wettersten, S. Rudolph, K. Faul, K. Gallagher, B. Trang, K. Adams, S. Graham, and C. Terrance, "Freedom through Self-Sufficiency: A Qualitative Examination of the Impact of Violence on the Working Lives of Women in Shelter," *Journal of Counseling Psychology* 51 (2004): 447–462.

28. S. Lloyd and N. Taluc, "The Effects of Male Violence on Female Employment," *Violence against Women* 5 (1999): 370–392.

29. E. Kelley and J. Mullen, "Organizational Response to Workplace Violence," in *Handbook of Workplace Violence*, ed. E. K. Kelloway, J. Barling, and J. Hurrell (New York: Sage, 2006).

30. See U.S. Department of Labor, Occupational Safety and Health Administration, http://www.osha.gov.

# CHAPTER 7

1. E. Kelley and J. Mullen, "Organizational Response to Workplace Violence," in *Handbook of Workplace Violence*, ed. K. Kelloway, J. Barling, and J. Hurrell (New York: Sage, 2006).

2. See U.S. Department of Labor, Occupational Safety and Health Administration, http://www.osha.gov.

3. D. Chappell and V. DeMartino, *Violence at Work* (Geneva, Switzerland: International Labor Office, 1998).

4. E. A. Rugala and A. R. Isaacs, *Workplace Violence: Issues in Response*, Federal Bureau of Investigation, 2006, http://www.fbi.gov/publications/violence.pdf.

5. Association of Federal, State, County, and Municipal Employees (AFSCME), "Identifying Workplace Violence Hazards," 2006, http://www.afscme.org/healthy/violtc.htm.

6. California Occupational Safety and Health Administration (Cal/OSHA), "Guidelines for Workplace Security," http://www.hr.ucdavis.edu/Elr/Er/Violence/Brochure.

7. Occupational Safety and Health Administration, *Guidelines for Preventing Workplace Violence for Health Care and Social Service Workers*, (OSHA3148–01R 2000), http:// www.osha.gov.

8. M. R. Stewart and B. H. Kleiner, "How to Curb Workplace Violence," *Facilities* 15 (1997): 5–11.

9. C. Fazzi, "How ADR Can Help Keep the Workplace Safe," *Dispute Resolution Journal* (May–July 2000).

10. R. Nydegger, "Violence, Aggression and Passive-Aggression in the Workplace," *Management Development Forum* 3 (2000): 89–96.

11. J. Hurrell, "Critical Incident Stress Debriefing and Workplace Violence," in *Handbook of Workplace Violence*, ed. E. K. Kelloway, J. Barling, and J. Hurrell (New York: Sage, 2006).

12. A. Schat and E. K. Kelloway, "Training as a Workplace Aggression Intervention Strategy," in *Handbook of Workplace Violence*, eds. E. K. Kelloway, J. Barling, and J. Hurrell (New York: Sage, 2006).

# Index

## About the Authors

MICHELE A. PALUDI is President of Human Resource Management Solutions, consulting and providing training to a wide array of corporations, educational institutions, and national organizations. Also an Adjunct Full Professor in the Department of Psychology at Union College and the Graduate College, Union University, she has published over twenty books, including *The Psychology of Sexual Victimization* (Praeger, 1999) and the *Praeger Guide to the Psychology of Gender* (Praeger, 2004), and 130 articles, chapters, and conferences presentations on issues of sexual harassment, gender role identity, human resource management, career development, and the psychology of work.

RUDY V. NYDEGGER is Professor of Psychology at Union College and Professor of Administration and Management at the School of Management, Union University. He also teaches in the Cornell University Institute of Industrial and Labor Relations and serves as Chief, Division of Psychology, Ellis Hospital. He has written dozens of professional and academic articles on issues of social psychology, consulted to major corporations and health care institutions, run workshops, and participated in conferences in the U.S. and abroad.

CARMEN A. PALUDI JR. is a Senior Scientific Advisor for Titan Systems Corporation and consults with Human Resource Management Solutions in the areas of computer- and web-based training and investigatory procedures for sexual harassment. He is the author of dozens of technical papers and reports and is co-editor, with Michele Paludi, of *Academic and Workplace Sexual Harassment* (Praeger, 2003).